Expanding Your World

Modeling the Structure of Experience

David Gordon

Graham Dawes

Desert Rain

For information, contact:
David Gordon, P.O. Box 42281, Tucson AZ 85733.
www.expandyourworld.net

ISBN: 0-9765616-0-3

To Leslie,

For her passionate and sincere explorations into the heart of experience
For her cherishing the hearts she discovered
For teaching us to do the same

Contents

Acknowledgements

It takes much more than two guys zinging document files back and forth across the Atlantic to create a book like this. All of our ideas and models were tested in the experience of many other people. We are therefore especially grateful to the participants in our seminars in Austin, Chicago, Denver, London, New York, Paris, and Tucson who contributed so significantly to this work:

Olivier Aba
Barbara Allison
Kathy Amy-Koempel
Nicole France Bahuet
Kay Baker
Diane Banta
Kerstin Barkman
Meme Bennett
Robert Beren
Dee Berridge
Jean-Gérard Bloch
Klaus Boettcher
Marjan Bolmeijer
Leslie Bosch
Mike Bown
David Brakefield
Brigid Breckman
Philip Brew
Kaaren Brook
Fred Brown
Jeffrey M. Brown
Virginia Brubaker
Carl Buchheit
Tony Buckley
Virgil Buell
Tom Carroll
Cynthia Cauthern
Jim Chenoweth
Alain Chevet
Barry Chiu
Françoise Cicurel
Gordon Clare
George Cocker
John Considine
Anne Constantin
Julie Davis
Sophie de Bryas
Jennifer de Gandt
Frances Deponio
Tom Doherty
Kevin Duane
Jenny Edwards
Patrick Elies
Rita Erickson
Mary-Beth Esser Ui Bhraonain
Phil Faris
Nichola Farnum
John Farrin

Michael Federick
Glen Friedman
Kay Frunzi
Anne Fuller-Good
Petros Geroulanos
Rachel Gibbin
Beth Haggarty
Michael Halbfish
David Hall
Tom Heaney
Steve Herridge
Terry Hickey
Jo Hogg
Katie Hogg
Gail Hurt
Derek Jackson
Chuck Jaeger
Robin Jarvis
Bob Kalman
Linda Kalman
Tim Keating
John Killman
Harlan Kilstein
Fred Klarer
Jack Klemeyer
Larry Koeppen
Grazyna Koperniak
Diane Kramer
Eric Kunze
Ingrid Kunze
Jo Ann Larson
Simon Laurie
James Lawley
Stephen Leeds
Tim Leishman
Phillipe Lemaire
Dan Lewis
Aude Limet
Harry Lundell
Edward Mark
Sushaan Maroli
Marron Martinique
Maria Sandhya Matthews
Douglas Mau
Virginie Mayolle
Ofer Melnik
Joan Mencher
Suzie Morel
Dan Moren

Dana Morey
Karman Morey
David Morelli
Silvia Nava
Steve Nuttall
Doug O'Brien
Don Palmer
Neil Parr
Claire Petitmengin-Peugeot
Janet Pevsner
Patricia Philbin
Carley Phillips
Christian Porret
Lori Postma
Bev Powell
Pierre Quettier
Vince Racioppo
Bill Raineri
Trudy Raschkind-Steinfeld
Jonathan Rice
Peter Rock
Ruth Roosevelt
Anne-Marie Roques
Sylvie Roussillon
Melissa Ryan
Laurel Sanford
Steve Scheetz
Gail Schiesser
Rob Schwartz
Serena Scrine
Lou Solarte
Patricia Solliers
David Sosebee
Kailash Sozzoni
Lou Stachura
Andrea Stallworth-Rice
Stephen Stanley
Peter Stokes
Kendall Summerhawk
Jim Swingle
Laz Temimi
Rita Thomson
Scott Thomson
John Walsh
Lindi Watts
Elizabeth White
Rachel Zahn
Richard Zayas

The modeling seminars these people attended were sponsored by individuals who believe in the field we are developing, and in us. So thank you: Metha Singleton (Center for Advanced Training), Klaus Boettcher, Virginia Brubaker and Gail Schiesser (NLP Institute of Chicago), Andrea Stallworth-Rice and Jonathan Rice (NLP of Austin), Tom Dotz (NLP Comprehensive), Jo Hogg (Metacommunications), Jennifer de Gandt (NLP Sans Frontièrs), and Steven Leeds and Rachel Hott (NLP Center of New York).

We extend our deepest appreciation to Dr. Ulrike Brandenburg, Lenny Calandrino, Terry Hickey, Judith Lowe, Gill Norman-Bruce, Barry, and Bob Smith, talented folks all, who graciously served as exemplars during the preparation of this book. Dana "border collie" Roberts and Paul Gordon helped in editing the manuscript, painstaking service for which we are also most grateful.

Most especially we want to thank Kendall and Kathy, who generously shared their experiences with us as exemplars–and as people–in the DVD.

D G
G D

"Being Passionate About Something"

Throughout the book and accompanying DVD we will be using the ability of "Being passionate about something" as our principal modeling example. The DVD portrays the process of forming a model, and sections transcribed from the DVD are used in the book to illustrate the various steps along the way. Having this experiential thread running through the DVD and book will help us understand and tie the together the various elements of modeling.

Our choice of "Being passionate about something" as the ability to model came from asking a number of people what ability, if they were to acquire it, would make a big difference in their lives. The results of this straw poll constellated around the theme of motivation. People mentioned two types of motivation; that of being motivated to do things they do not want to do (tax returns, for instance), and that of being motivated to do things they *do* want to do but are *still* not doing. The phrase often associated with this latter type of motivation was "I want to feel *passionate* about something." This is what we chose to model, on the grounds that the more passionate we are about something the more likely we are to engage in it, and to enjoy engaging in it. Additionally, we can become motivated to do even those things we do *not* want to do (but need to do) if we can see how they link to something that *is* a passion of ours.

Our *exemplar*–a person who excels at an ability–for this exploration is Kendall, someone who well knows what it is to be passionate about things.

Using the Companion DVD

Modeling is much more than a set of concepts; it is a dynamic and interactive process occurring between you and another person. In order to bring to life the concepts and processes in this book, we have created a companion DVD. The DVD provides demonstrations of actually coming to grips with the full process of modeling. In addition, in order to make the written descriptions of the process of modeling more concrete for you, we have used the DVD demonstrations as our primary source of process examples in the text. This allows you to go from reading about a process to watching it take place on the DVD or, alternatively, to go from viewing the DVD to reading about that portion of the modeling process here in the text.

We have a few suggestions regarding the most helpful sequence for observing the three parts of the DVD:

Part I is a demonstration of the process of Elicitation (the gathering of information). We recommend watching Part I before reading the chapters that cover Elicitation (Chapters 5–11). This will make it easier for you to follow the process of modeling as we explore it in detail in those seven chapters. In addition, because the text examples come from the DVD demonstration, you will be able to connect what you are reading with something that you have seen and heard yourself. You will also find it very useful to watch the Elicitation segment once again after reading Chapters 5–11.

Part II is an illustration of Refining the information you have gathered during Elicitation. In this segment we return to Kendall in order to clarify certain points about her ability. Again, in order to make the text more real and meaningful, we suggest that you watch Part II before reading Chapter 13 on the process of Refining the model. And again, we suggest reviewing Part II after reading Chapter 13.

Part III is a demonstration of Acquisition, that is, of helping someone acquire the ability we modeled in Parts I and II. Unlike those segments, we recommend watching Part III *after* reading the chapter on Acquisition (Chapter 14). Watching the demonstration after reading Chapter 14 will make the Acquisition process much more understandable and useful.

Preface

"Actually, what I'm *really* good at is making love."

The effect of Barry's words on the participants in our modeling seminar was the same as that of a magnet dropped into the midst of scattered iron filings: instant alignment. Following lines of invisible and irresistible forces, the previously jumbled roomful of people instantly oriented to Barry. All eyes fixed upon him and followed his every movement as he gently swiveled from side to side atop a barstool. Barry smiled shyly at us. He was the only person in the room still breathing.

Every person is a repository of both delightful and useful human abilities. Furthermore, the set of abilities that each of us possesses is only a portion of the infinite kaleidoscope of abilities to be found among humankind as a whole. The authors' goal—our passion—has been to explore those abilities, to discover new experiential territories for ourselves, and to learn how to open those same territories to others. We explore these territories of experience through *modeling*.

Modeling is a process of transferring the ability of an "exemplar"—a person who is particularly good at doing something—to the modeler. For example, a modeler who wants to "create successful marketing programs" will identify the significant patterns of experience and behavior operating in someone who is excellent at creating such programs. The modeler then uses those patterns to replicate that same ability in herself. This book is about learning the perceptual and interactional skills needed to identify and acquire significant patterns of experience; that is, to do modeling.

The participants in the modeling training with Barry had been working long and hard to acquire those skills. We wanted to give them the opportunity to test themselves with someone from outside the group, someone fresh. After a few inquiries we had snared two volunteers, Joseph and Barry. This would allow us to divide the seminar into two smaller information-gathering groups, providing more opportunities for participation. In addition, for the investment of the same amount of time, we would end up with two models. We began by perching Joseph and Barry in front of the group to ask them a few general questions.

Joseph was there to share his unique ability to make speculative investments that result in returns of 40% or more. The possibility of making a lot of money through investments certainly put an avid gleam in many an eye in the group.

In Barry's case, we were set to model his ability to plan a project, a gift that held him in good stead in his work as a professional carpenter. As we asked for examples of his planning abilities, Barry grew uncomfortable. He finally confessed that he thought there was something he was much better at than planning. That was when he admitted, "Actually, what I'm *really* good at is making love."

Barry's ability to plan projects dropped off our neural radar screens in an instant and forever. We asked him a number of questions to assure ourselves that there was some basis for his claim, then sent him and Joseph to separate rooms to await their modelers. After our participants pondered their choices for three or four nanoseconds, the stampede for Barry's room was on. A few participants joined Joseph, but only after being reassured that what was discovered in Barry's room would be shared with the entire group later.

For the next two hours Barry gamely answered questions from the semi-circle of eager men and women. This is some of what we heard:

> "I'm willing to release any kind of barriers to be in a relationship... My being open fosters openness and vulnerability in the woman... The result is not just a sexual experience but a powerful emotional experience. *That's* what I like and choose in any kind of relationship."

> "The being in love thing is *so* misunderstood. To me it means both of us showing up as who we are, no pretenses, no facades, not holding back, giving all of who you are, one hundred percent."

> "I can't drag someone there... Recognition and willingness to go there are crucial because the will to do it is a large part of having it be done. If there's a willingness to enter in, a synergy develops."

> "I treat her like someone I've never met. I don't know what will please her—the process of *discovering* is so much fun... What I do then is begin a process of putting myself in the woman's experience with the desired outcome of a form of giving... I want to give her an experience of me and experience of herself that she hasn't had before... It's a process of discovery... No rules, no specific direction. With *that* in place it doesn't matter

if anything happens. It's a goal-less moment. An unforgettable sexual experience has nothing to do with orgasm."

"Vulnerability is a big one. Some pretty primal emotions I have difficulty putting words on that have to do with safety and security—just feeling so *safe and protected* in the midst of open and vulnerable."

"It certainly stimulates a sense of well-being in me, a sense of belonging, of meaningfulness. I experience my life has meaning. There's nothing in that moment more important... There isn't anywhere else to go. It's an acknowledgment you are in process."

"The important thing again is the connection... experience that connection."

And so it went. For two hours he shared with us his world when making love. Undoubtedly, many of us in that room had secretly harbored the hope that Barry would reveal *The 3 Tricks to Being a Great Lover.* Barry had no such bag of tricks. Nor did he have *The 7 Habits of Highly Successful Satyrs, The 10 Secrets of Sexual Ecstasy,* or *The 14-Day Perfect Sex Plan.*

As we explored Barry's experience and behavior it soon became evident that, for him, being good at making love is not simply a matter of knowing what to do. It is not the result of mood music, murmured endearments, or a skillfully executed list of whizbang moves. Being a great lover is much more than that for Barry. And much deeper.

For Barry, being a good lover is the result of an intricate web of perceptions, experiences, and behaviors. We heard about external behaviors ("eye contact... I have an intensity and I show I have that..."), feelings ("joy, liberation"), strategies ("I also ask myself about making love to a woman as a woman. I put myself into that. A woman would know how to make love to another woman."), and beliefs ("Everyone has the intuition what it would be to [fall in love]. That's what we're here for, though we hold ourselves back"). He told us what mattered to him and why.

We were nearing the end of the interview when someone suggested that Barry and his partner "have a willingness to go to that special place," and then they just go there. As if grabbing the arm of a friend who was about to step off the curb into oncoming traffic, Barry jerked forward:

"It doesn't just *happen.* I move myself there. It's an action I take. I believe that the magic of falling in love is due to a belief that I *can* and *do*. And if people fall out of love it's because they've chosen to not make romance stay."

In speaking those words, Barry was throwing down the gauntlet of modeling: That it is possible to *choose* to manifest any human ability. This is a notion with far-reaching implications. This is a notion that challenges us, a notion that conjures possibilities and casts an inquiring light into the cupboards of arcana where we store human potentials for generativity, paradigmatic shifts, and the evolution of consciousness. *Can* we—can anyone—learn to make romance stay? Or effectively negotiate, tell a joke, empathize with others, manage a large group, compose music, write a book, promptly pay bills, be thrilled by an abstract painting, plan the future, learn from the past, or ease the fears of a child?

Can we learn from Barry or anyone else how they do what they do, and then make those abilities a reality in our own lives?

This book is an answer to that question. We are about to pick up the gauntlet of modeling... and discover some of what we are made of.

1

What Is Modeling?

All of us dream of being able to do things that we cannot do now. Our dreams may be reactions to deficiencies we believe we have, or they may flow from our being inspired about what is *possible* to do. We see other people fluently speaking a foreign language, playing a commanding game of chess, enjoying solitude, capturing the imagination of struggling students, being organized, sticking to an exercise regimen, or living out some personal passion and ask, "Why not me, too?"

Of course, some people are born with certain talents. Obvious examples are the child prodigies who excel at music, mathematics, or chess. Not so obvious, but no less prodigious, are children born with the ability to easily make friends, or keep focused on a task, or enjoy dancing. Even people who are not prodigies can nevertheless play beautiful music, solve difficult math problems, play masterful chess, make friends easily, stay focused, or enjoy dancing. They learned to do these things. In fact, most of our abilities were learned in the course of living our lives. Without our intending or perhaps even noticing it, our life experiences have taught us many things. And some of us learned to do certain things very well.

Our life experiences teach us particular patterns of perceiving, thinking, and behaving; one set of patterns is good for learning a foreign language, another for making sound investments, another for making a friend, and so on. If there is an ability that you lack, it is not because you do not have the capacity to have it; you simply missed out on those life experiences that would have taught you the patterns of perceiving, thinking, and behaving needed for that ability.

Modeling, then, is the process of identifying and describing in a useful way those patterns that make up a particular ability. Once we know the patterns, we can make them our own and begin to manifest the ability.

Janet Pevsner (a participant in one of our seminars) offered us a wonderful example of the possibilities of modeling. In her work as a speech therapist she uses drawing as a way to help her students learn self-monitoring and self-correction skills. The students begin by taking ten minutes to draw their own copy of a line drawing she shows them. She then spends five minutes teaching them *how to look* at what they are drawing. Janet's "how to" comes from modeling work done by artist Dr. Betty Edwards. As an art teacher, Edwards was baffled by the fact that some students readily learned to draw while others seemed to never "get it":

> "Well," I would say carefully, "you look at the still-life and you draw it as you see it." "I was looking at it," the student replied. "I just don't know how to draw that." "Well," I would say, voice rising, "you just *look* at it..." The response would come, "I *am* looking at it," and so on.[1]

Demonstration and encouragement produced little success. Edwards looked deeper, exploring how those who can draw well are seeing and thinking about their subjects. The result was a model that in turn generated a set of techniques that make drawing an acquirable skill for anyone.

This is the same model for drawing that Janet spends five minutes teaching her young students. After five additional minutes of reassessing their first drawing, the children take ten minutes more to make a second drawing. A few examples of the results can be seen in Figure 1.[2]

For these children, having a new model for thinking and perceiving made a world of difference in their ability to draw. There are many other well-known examples of modeling. In the world of business, for instance, Peter Senge modeled "learning organizations," which could then be implemented through "disciplines" (ways of thinking about and conducting business). In the world of self-help, Stephen Covey modeled "the seven habits" of people who are highly effective at the things they do. Robert McKee modeled successful film scripts, and teaches that model to thousands of writers through books and seminars. And Richard Bandler and John Grinder—under the name Neuro-Linguistic Programming—profoundly influenced the practice of psychotherapy with their modeling of masterful therapists such as Fritz Perls, Virginia Satir, and Milton H. Erickson.

You don't need to wait for someone else to do your modeling for you, however. Modeling is something that anyone can learn to do. It is a skill that allows you to do some deep and effective learning from anyone who has an ability you would like to have for yourself or make available to others.

Many people who have been through our modeling trainings have done

---

[1] Betty Edwards, *The New Drawing on the Right Side of the Brain*, p. XI.

[2] Our thanks to Tim Kato, Eric Olearczyk, and Andy Sarley for permission to reproduce their drawings.

Figure 1.

just that. For example, Steve Nuttall (with his associate, Celia MacDonald) modeled self-managing teams working on North Sea oil rigs to discover what made some teams particularly effective and cohesive. Harlan Kilstein modeled tough negotiators, and used their patterns himself (as well as teaching other people to use them) to come out ahead in hostile salary negotiations. Tim Leishman used his models of the various roles played by lawyers in law firms to help them get the most out of their partnerships. Dee Berridge produced models covering three essential aspects of consulting for an international public relations firm, models that were then turned into training programs for 250 people in 13 countries. Tom Heaney modeled the ability to extend Ch'i ("life force"), then taught it to his martial arts students. Mark Tier wrote a book that makes his model of investors Warren Buffet and George Soros easily accessible. Applying her modeling skills to working with horses, Liz Morrison wrote a series of books on riding. And Tom Carroll, Robin Jarvis, Beverly Powell, and Mike Bown occupy an enviable position as the in-house modeling and training group for a semiconductor consortium.

What is a Model?

When we want to go somewhere we use a map. A map identifies significant aspects of a particular area—streets, public buildings, parks, mountains, rivers—and shows us how those elements relate to each other. We can then use this map to guide us in choosing where to go and how to get there. Similarly, architects create blueprints, which are models that guide the builders through the construction of a building, and dressmakers create paper patterns that guide the cutting and piecing together of material into a dress.

Models of human experience and abilities are much like maps, blueprints, and dress patterns; they describe the elements, patterns, and relationships that are characteristic of a particular ability.

But not all descriptions are equal, just as not all maps are equal. A useful map is one that gives us the information we need to get where we want to go. Similarly, a model is *useful* if it helps us reproduce in our *own* experience and behavior an ability that someone else has. The question is, "Does the model work for me?" That is the test of a useful model.

Why Model?

As we said, most of our individual abilities were learned through our life experiences. Through trial and error, through instruction, through correction and reinforcement, we learned to use language, understand the nuances of social interactions, ride a bicycle, do algebra, behave ethically, study, work hard, entertain, and tell a joke. In every case, we needed to learn the perceptions, patterns of thinking, and behaviors necessary to operate effectively in that particular context.

Much of what we learned probably came from emulating people who impressed or inspired us in some way. Whether it was a mother, father, grandparent, sibling, teacher, neighbor, or even a character in a movie or book, you probably consciously and unconsciously tried to emulate that person's appearance, patterns of speech, and behavior. You tried to say things the way that person said them, do what she did, read what she read, make the choices she made, think the way she thought.

Why, then, do we need to create a formal modeling process for the acquisition of abilities?

The primary reason is that the informal modeling that all of us engage in is haphazard; what we learn depends for the most part upon our discovering in the masses of information offered to us those elements of experience and behavior essential to manifesting the ability. Of 30 children in a classroom learning to draw, some will "get it" and others will not. As Edwards' work demonstrates, being able to draw is not a genetic endowment, but an ability made possible by having the necessary underlying perceptions and concepts. Those children who "get" drawing either walk in the door with those underlying perceptions and concepts, or are able to intuit and absorb them from the descriptions and examples given by the teacher. For other children, those same descriptions and examples do not generate the necessary perceptions and concepts. For them, drawing remains mysterious and unattainable.

Imagine instead that the drawing teacher has an explicit understanding—a model—of the essential patterns of perception that make it possible to draw (perhaps using Edwards' model). And further imagine that the first thing the teacher does is to make sure that all of the students have access to those patterns of perception. Having those underlying perceptions does not mean that suddenly the students will be drawing beautifully; what it does mean is that now they *can learn* to draw beautifully. All of them.

Modeling provides quicker, easier, and surer access to desired abilities.

Why Modeling is Possible

Human experience is organized at very subtle levels. Many examples of this subtlety can be found in Edward T. Hall's books, in which he explores our experiences of time and space. In *The Dance of Life*, for instance, he describes fascinating experiments by Alton De Long on the influence of scale on our perception of time. De Long created rooms that were full scale, and $1/6^{th}$, $1/12^{th}$, and $1/24^{th}$ scale, then had his subjects project themselves into these test rooms and imagine interacting with the human figurines he had placed in them. The subjects indicated when they thought 30 minutes had passed, while De Long kept track of the actual time. The result was that subjects who were "in" the $1/6^{th}$ scale room experienced 60 minutes of subjective experience in *10 minutes*. In the $1/12^{th}$ scale room, five minutes elapsed for a subjective 60-minute period, and two and a half minutes elapsed in the $1/24^{th}$ scale room.[3]

A variation of this experience is familiar to all of us: Compare how long a journey seems to you the first time you take it with how long it seems the second, third, and fourth times. The first time offers many new details to notice per minute. These packed minutes seem longer. However, as the details become more familiar with each subsequent journey we notice fewer of them per minute, the minutes contract, and the journey seems shorter (or quicker). (You can test out this effect the next time you take a very familiar journey. As you pass through the familiar area, intentionally notice as much new detail as you can; the journey will seem longer to you.)

Sensory perception is not the only area of our experience in which we find formative patterns. We find patterns operating in our beliefs, cognition, and behavior as well. And just as with perceptions, these patterns determine to a great extent the experiences we have and the abilities we enjoy.

For example, during World War II, Viktor Frankl was a prisoner in Nazi concentration camps. His body had been confined, but not his mind. In his book *Man's Search for Meaning*, Frankl has profound and moving things to say about his experiences and what it means to be a human being in such horrific circumstances. In particular, he tried to understand how it was that some prisoners seemed to give up hope (and usually soon thereafter died), while others persevered, maintaining hope in the face of constant physical, emotional, and psychological battering (even when facing the likelihood of death). Frankl recognized four patterns that were characteristic of those who continued to hope in a seemingly hopeless situation.

The first of these patterns was believing that whatever has been lost could be regained, that "health, family, happiness, professional abilities, fortune, position in society—all these were things that could be achieved again or restored" (Frankl, p.103). The second pattern those who continued to hope shared was that of realizing that the future was unknowable and, so, could in an instant bring about significant changes—including *good* changes—in their situation. Frankl describes the third pattern:

---

[3] Edward T. Hall, The Dance of Life, pp. 136-138.

But I did not only talk [to my fellow prisoners] of the future and the veil which was drawn over it. I also mentioned the past; with all its joys, and how its light shone even in the present darkness. Again I quoted a poet—to avoid sounding like a preacher myself—who had written, "Was Du erlebt, kann keine Macht der Welt Dir rauben." (What you have experienced, no power on earth can take from you.) Not only our experiences, but all we have done, whatever great thoughts we may have had, and all we have suffered, all this is not lost, though it is past; we have brought it into being. Having been is also a kind of being, and perhaps the surest kind. (Frankl, p.104)

The fourth pattern characteristic of those who continued to hope was that they maintained a compelling future, a future in which they were responsible for something or someone and, so, had to live to fulfill that responsibility:

A man who becomes conscious of the responsibility he bears toward a human being who affectionately waits for him, or to an unfinished work, will never be able to throw away his life. He knows the "why" for his existence, and will be able to bear almost any "how." (Frankl, p.101)

The four patterns of believing and thinking that Frankl identified—to believe that what has been lost can be regained, that the future is unknowable, that one's past experiences are not lost, and the ability to hold a compelling future—together constitute the *structure* underlying the ability to hold on to hope when one is in a horrible situation. What do we mean by "structure?"

STRUCTURE AND EXPERIENCE

A pile of bricks, window frames, and doors is not a house. Neither is a blueprint a house. A house is what happens when the bricks, windows, and doors are organized in relation to one another according to the structure described by the blueprint. Similarly, a model specifies how to structure our experience in order to have ("build") a particular ability.

In fact, we can look at any human ability and find that there is an underlying structure that gives rise to it. You can test this out for yourself with a small experiment: Select one of your own abilities—for instance, the ability to dance gracefully, or to find solutions to business problems, or to enjoy making cold calls, or to explain math to children—and identify just one important belief you hold when you are manifesting that ability. (For example, if you are good at explaining math to children, you might believe that "Every child is capable of learning.") Now imagine you are in that context, but this time you are holding a belief that is *opposite* to the one you identified. (In our example, you would imagine explaining math to a child while believing that "***Not*** every child is capable of learning.") Notice in what ways changing that one belief dramatically changes your experience.

What happened to your ability when you "flipped" one of your beliefs? You probably found yourself feeling somewhat different, making different assessments in the situation, saying different things, and doing things differently. In fact, inverting that one belief may have entirely undermined your ability.

With a moment of further reflection you can find additional examples from your own personal history of when a single change in what you believed, how you thought, or how you behaved led to a cascade of changes in the structure of your experience and in your personal world. All of us have had many such experiences. Most of them were trivial, but some of them were profound, initiating a cascade of changes. For instance, when a colleague of ours was eight years old, a friend asked her, "Do you still believe in Santa Claus?" Until that moment, it had not occurred to her that Santa Claus was not real. And beyond that, it was the first time she realized that there was such a thing as "believing in something." After that, "truth" became distinct from "belief," and what was so could no longer be taken for granted. A dramatic change had been made in the structure of her experience.

In modeling, *"structure" refers to the set of patterns of experience that give rise to a particular ability.* As soon as we recognize that it is the structure of experience that gives rise to our various abilities, then manifesting new abilities by intentionally acquiring their underlying structures becomes a real possibility. And this is what we are doing when we model.

2

The Experiential Array

One afternoon in a small town in Denmark, we were crossing a bridge with a friend of ours. We stopped halfway across to admire the gently rippling, gray-green waters below. At least that is how the water appeared to us. Then our friend (a painter) remarked on the lovely pinks. Our first response was, "*Pink?* What are you talking about?" Then she showed us where to look, and how to look. We began to see the pink, too. In fact, it became obvious. Indeed, from that time on, we were able to notice pink (and other unexpected colors) whenever we looked at bodies of water. Our friend had helped us make a distinction in our perception of colors in water.

A *distinction* is a marking out of something—an object, perception, experience, idea—as being somehow distinctive. We make many distinctions in our world. A chair is not the same thing as a stool. Historical novels, autobiographies, thrillers, mysteries, graphic novels, fantasies, and science fiction are distinctive kinds of books. *Sea green* is distinct from *pea green.* We recognize that *loving* is somewhat different than being *in love*, and that being *smart* is not quite the same as being *clever* (or *knowledgeable* or *intelligent*). Marking something out in this way separates it from the infinitely rich world we live in, bringing it into the foreground of our awareness. This process of marking out is significant because it is only when we are aware of something that we can intentionally respond to it and interact with it.

Because the world is infinitely rich we cannot—and do not want to—respond to everything. A map of the United States that contained all the information that *could* be mapped would have to be as big as the United States itself (at least!). A map never describes everything that is true of the terrain it covers. It is the intended use of the map that determines the particular kinds of information it portrays. A vacation map shows us roads, cities, campgrounds, and national parks; it does not help us decide where to start a wheat farm. In order to select a good place to farm we need a map that shows areas of annual rainfall, seasonal temperatures, and soil composition. As these map examples illustrate, our choice of distinctions is crucial because our distinctions determine what of this infinite world is brought into our awareness.

Like a map, a model does not describe everything about an ability. It describes only those elements of experience that are essential in order to have the ability working in us; a model that does that is a *useful* model. We have found that the primary distinctions essential for usefully modeling human abilities are:

Beliefs	Guiding ideas about meanings and causes
Strategies	Effective patterns of thinking and behavior
Emotions	Influential feeling states
External Behaviors	Significant behaviors, movements, facial expressions, verbalizations, and voice tonalities

These four elements of experience are significant to varying degrees, depending upon the particular ability we are considering. For example, creating a comedy monologue may rely heavily on Strategies and very little on External Behavior, but *delivering* a comedy monologue may rely more on External Behavior and less on Strategies. No matter what the ability is, however, there will always be some contribution and interaction of Beliefs, Strategies, Emotions, and External Behaviors. It is the combination of these elements of experience that give rise to the Ability.

To help us record and keep track of these elements of experience when eliciting a model, we use the Experiential Array[1]:

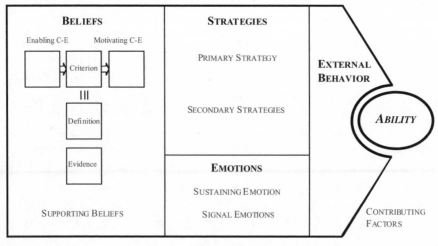

Figure 2

---

[1] As you can see, the Array includes distinctions in addition to the four primary ones we have already made; we will introduce these finer distinctions as we go along.

The Array simplifies the process of elicitation by offering specific places to put each element of experience as we gather information. This helps make obvious both what we already know about the exemplar's experience and what elements of their experience we still need to explore.

Flow of Effect

The Array is more than just a repository for information; that is a function that could be served as well by any number of other formats. The Array also captures some of the *dynamics of the system*. All the elements of experience interact simultaneously to make possible the expression of an ability. This does not mean that they necessarily exert equal influence on each other. Instead, there is a *flow of effect*. Typically, your thoughts and feelings have a greater impact on your behavior than your behavior has on your thoughts and feelings. Likewise, your beliefs generally have a greater impact on what you think, feel, and do than what you think, feel, and do have on what you believe at a moment in time.

You probably have many personal examples of this flow of effect. Examples that tend to be revealing are those in which you tried to change your behavior even though what you were believing in that situation had not changed. (For instance, your attempt to be nice to a relative who you believed was habitually interfering in your life.) If you were able to change your behavior at all, you probably had to be vigilant about it in order to maintain that change in behavior. Also, your change in behavior probably did not last through time. This is in contrast to times when you have changed what you *believed*, which immediately and naturally led to permanent changes in your behavior. (For instance, your behavior might well change when you suddenly realize that your nosy relative is not at all intent on interfering, but is actually simply being protective.)

Keep in mind that the flow of effect refers to what is going on in experience at the time an Ability is being manifested. While you are manifesting an Ability the flow of effect is generally from Beliefs toward External Behavior (Figure 3).

The notion of flow of effect reminds us that simply engaging in behavior may not in and of itself be sufficient to manifest an Ability. Behind the *natural* manifestation of those behaviors are supportive ways of thinking and feeling, and behind them all are supportive beliefs. It is the dynamic relationship between all of these elements that gives rise to the Ability.

In fact, the Ability is the dynamic relationship between all of these

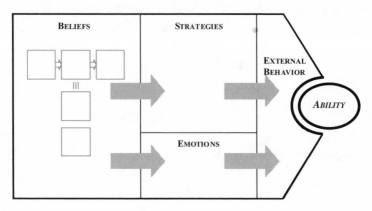

Figure 3

elements. This is why there is no arrow in the diagram going to "Ability." In fact, "Ability" is not even joined to the rest of the Array; the Ability is the *whole* of the Array. That is, when the elements of experience are "there" and operating, so is the Ability.

Even so, in the Array we put the Ability in close relationship to External Behavior. This is because it is usually through external behaviors that an ability is manifested, and it is certainly through external behaviors that the world is affected by an ability. For example, the ability to motivate students, or to make shrewd investments, or to stay on a diet all involve numerous beliefs, states, and strategies. All of these internal structures must be manifested in behavior, however, for them to have an impact on those students, that bank account, or that waistline.

3

The Process

Being clear about your destination helps ensure that you actually get there. The first (and perhaps most important) step of your modeling journey is to specify what you want to model. Being clear about what ability you want will help you find expert guides—your exemplars. Exemplars are people who *already know* the way there.

The process of modeling begins by answering the question:

"What do I want to be able to do?"

When answering this question remember that the quality of our lives is largely determined by the small and typically unsung human abilities that fill the many moments of our days. There are people who bounce back from disappointments. There are others who are good at telling jokes. There are those who can be delighted by an abstract painting, and those who respond to criticism as an opportunity to learn something about themselves. Some know how to explain things clearly, others conscientiously care for their bodies, and there are people who can take time to warm themselves in a shaft of sunlight. Still others maintain their values in challenging situations, or feel an ongoing sense of meaning in their lives, or can connect with their teenage children. You can even find people who enjoy talking in front of groups.

The people who have these abilities often do not recognize them as anything special or worthy of modeling. To them their abilities are NOT special: "It's just what I do." For you, however, their abilities may be very special, and just what you need.

Every ability is a means to an end; that is, it has some effect or outcome. Often when we think of what we want, we put our attention on that outcome and not on the *doing* that makes that outcome possible. It is the difference between saying, "I want to get an 'A' in chemistry" (the outcome) and "I want to learn chemistry" (the *doing* that can lead to an 'A'); the difference between "I want to be a leader" and "I want to lead by inspiring and motivating people at work"; the difference between "I want to have harmony with my spouse" and "I want to communicate well with my spouse." Notice that the initial modeling question asks, "What do I want to be able to *do*?" When you model, you are not acquiring a fish (the outcome), but learning how to fish (the Ability).

Be prepared to dig a bit deeper than your initial answer to the question, "What do I want to be able to do?" Suppose that you want to model how to write books. Does the answer, "I want to be able to write books" point you well enough in the direction you really want—and need—to go? Is writing technical books the same as writing non-fiction books for the mass market? Probably not. Is writing non-fiction the same as writing fiction? Again, probably not. Does writing in the various fiction genres—science fiction, mysteries, novels, children's books—require the same Ability? No, there are undoubtedly some different writing abilities involved in each of these forms, as well. The more specific you are about the Ability you want, the more likely you are to find an exemplar for *just* what you want to be able to do.

Sub-Abilities

Many Abilities are actually more usefully approached as a set of *sub-abilities*. Sub-abilities are smaller, constituent abilities that combine to make possible the larger Ability. For instance, it may be that the Ability to successfully write adolescent fiction involves the sub-abilities of Keeping current on the adolescent world, Formulating a plot, Creating characters, Writing text, Editing, and Interesting a publisher or agent. Each of these sub-abilities is a modelable ability in its own right, one that works together with its companion sub-abilities to create the global Ability (Writing adolescent fiction).

In looking at the sub-abilities, you may decide that there is only one (or perhaps a few) that you really need; the others are either not of interest to you or are ones you already have in some measure. For example, when it comes to Writing adolescent fiction, you may recognize that you are already adept at Keeping abreast of the adolescent world, as well as Creating characters. There is no need for you to model those abilities. And since you are interested only in writing stories to be given to your teenage children, there is also no need to model the ability to Interest publishers and agents. Perhaps what you DO need, however, are the abilities to Formulate a plot and to Edit. These, then, will be the Abilities you will want to have in focus as you gather information from your exemplar.

SELECTING EXEMPLARS

> Tesshu was acknowledged as a great swordsman. He also let it be
> known that he was a master of Zen as well. One day Tesshu paid a
> visit to Zen master Dokuon. With great pride, Tesshu told the old
> master that all that exists is empty, that there is no you, no me, and so
> on. The master listened in silence, then suddenly sprang forward with
> his tobacco pipe and smacked Tesshu on the head. Infuriated, Tesshu
> leapt to his feet, prepared to kill master Dokuon. Unfazed, Dokuon
> calmly observed, "Emptiness is quick to show its anger, isn't it?"
> Tesshu smiled and left the room.

Exemplars can come to your attention through your personal experience of
them, through recommendations from others, or through their own
declarations. Regardless of how you become aware of this person as an
exemplar, you need evidence of her competence. You need to satisfy yourself
that this person does in fact manifest the ability you want to model.

Once you have identified a possible exemplar, you can ask her to give you
examples of having manifested the ability. If possible, however, arrange to see
the exemplar in action. This is the best way to tell whether or not she
actually has the precise ability you want: If she is supposed to be excellent at
holding the attention of 13-year-olds, go to her class and watch her teach. If
she is supposed to be great at telling jokes, have her tell you some. If she is
known for responding to criticism as an opportunity to learn, criticize her. If
she writes screenplays, read some of them.

Direct experience of the exemplar manifesting her ability will also give
you a sense of the *manner* in which she manifests that ability. For example,
suppose you have two exemplars of good teaching, both of whose students are
clearly learning. One of these teachers, however, is a calm presence at the
front of a placid classroom, while the other teacher ricochets through the
classroom, a blur of energy and interaction. Both of these teachers can serve
as exemplars of excellent teaching and will undoubtedly share fundamental
patterns that make that ability possible. If, however, you want to model a calm
style of teaching, then the *first* exemplar is the one you will want to model. If
instead you prefer the energetic quality of the second teacher, then choose her
as your exemplar.

Framing for Exemplars

Some people are reticent when asked to be a modeling subject. If a person is reluctant to be an exemplar it is almost always because they do not see what they do as something special (and, so, not worthy of your time and effort) or because they are concerned that they do not know enough about how they do it (and, so, won't be able to tell you what you want to know). Both of these concerns can be addressed by simply telling your chosen exemplar the truth: First, that she is able to do something you admire, consider of great value, and want to understand well enough that you can do it too, and second, that she does not need to consciously know how she does what she does because it is *your* (the modeler's) job to ask those questions that help reveal how she does what she does.

Invariably, once the modeling begins, exemplars become completely engaged in the process; most of us find it fascinating to see how we are put together. You will find that your exemplar will quickly become a co-modeler with you, working hard to help you make sense out of her experience. In fact, it is almost always the case that exemplars report truly enjoying the experience of being modeled, finding it interesting, gratifying, and even ennobling.

Since successful modeling comes from collaboration, make your exemplar your collaborator. One of the most effective ways to foster this is by recording the information you are gathering in such a way that she can see how you are understanding and representing her experience. A flip chart works very well for this purpose (as do chalk and white boards, or even pieces of paper on the table turned so the exemplar can see them as the elicitation proceeds). Because the exemplar can see how she is being represented, she has the time and opportunity to consider her answers more fully. If your exemplar thinks you are off on a wrong track, she will probably correct you. After all, it is her experience that is being described, and all of us want to be described accurately. We have had our exemplars correct us countless times, and this is precisely what we want them to do.

We also suggest that you tape your modeling sessions. You can use the tape to review and to resolve questions that come to your mind afterwards regarding things you thought you understood at the time of the elicitation. In addition, having a tape will allow you to relax during the process, knowing that if you miss something you can listen to the recording later.

Elicitation

Observing your exemplar in action will be very instructive. However, because it is internal processes that are most responsible for generating those actions, you need to gain access to the internal world of your exemplar as well. This is done primarily through *elicitation*. Elicitation involves asking questions intended to help your exemplar notice, and report on, those elements of her internal experience that you need for your model.

It is not the exemplar's job to already know what you, the modeler, need to know about the structure of her experience; she just has it (and very likely never explored its structure before). Instead, it is your job to help your exemplar gain access to those aspects of her experience that may be significant. And you do this primarily through asking questions.

Asking Questions

Being asked a question is more than an experiential nudge that gets us moving; it is a nudge that gets us moving *in a particular direction*. Your questions set frames for your exemplar to think *through*. They are conceptual filters that set direction, opening up certain lines of thought and leaving others out of consciousness and unexplored. As an example, notice what happens in your thoughts and feelings when you ask yourself:

"What are the barriers to my personal development?"

Now ask yourself a somewhat different question and notice how it affects your thoughts and feelings:

"What are my opportunities for personal development?"

You probably discovered that each of these questions took your experience in different directions. The difference was not only in terms of what you were thinking about, but also in how you were feeling about yourself and your future. The "you" that you were asking did not change from question to question, but what you attended to *did* change. And this change was guided by the form and content of the two questions you asked.

The fact that questions suggest what is relevant—thereby setting the filters through which we perceive our experience—means that it matters what questions we use for elicitation. The differences in questions can be subtle, and yet significant. For example, suppose we are modeling a teacher. There is a significant difference between asking, "What were you feeling when you stood in front of the class?" and, "*As* you stand in front of the class, what *are* you feeling?" The past tense of the first question will tend to keep the teacher separate from her past experience (*looking back on* her experience); the present tense of the second question will tend to take our teacher *into the present of* her past experience. (You can test this in your own experience by asking yourself questions that take these two forms.)

In the chapters to come we will offer you elicitation questions that we have found effective in guiding an exemplar to the information you need. (Appendix II presents all of the elicitation questions in the Array format.) As good as those questions are, however, you cannot blindly depend upon them to automatically bring to the surface each of the elements of your exemplar's experience. No matter how pointed and refined your question is, your exemplar may respond with information that is either not an answer to your question, is incomplete, or is difficult to make sense of. The solution to this is *stepping in.*

Stepping In

Guided by our questions, the exemplar describes those aspects of her experience that we hope are relevant to our being able to reproduce her Ability. The most direct way to know whether or not the exemplar is offering us relevant information is by discovering how our *own* experience is affected by taking on those aspects of her experience. That is, we need to answer for *ourselves* the question :

> "Does adjusting my experience to match this element of the exemplar's experience take me closer toward manifesting her ability, or not?"

This question can be answered only *in* experience; it is not a matter of intellectual analysis. When it comes to the alchemy of experience, we must test the information we gather in the crucible of ourselves. It is there that we discover whether or not we are getting the elements we need from the exemplar. This process of taking on in ourselves the exemplar's structure of experience is called *stepping in.*

By taking on the exemplar's structure of experience as we step into the context in which the ability is needed, we can directly test in ourselves what is working for us and where we still need clarification. From *inside* the ability we can more readily identify where, for us, there are still holes in the structure.

For example, suppose we are modeling the ability to forgive. We learn from our exemplar that when she has been hurt by someone, she recognizes that "I, too, have made similar mistakes." But when we step into our exemplar's Ability and try to forgive a certain friend by recognizing that we "have made similar mistakes," we discover that it is not working for us. We realize that this friend hurt us *intentionally*; it was *not* a "mistake." By stepping in we have discovered that there is a hole in our model: "How do you forgive people who have hurt you intentionally?"

Bear in mind that ultimately you are modeling your exemplar in order to have the structure of her ability present and working in *you*. So that is where the quality and significance of the information you are gathering needs to be tested. And you do that by stepping in.

Patterning

But just what is it that you are looking for as you ask questions and step in, sifting through the layers of the exemplar's experience? You are looking for *patterns*. A pattern is two (or more) things that relate to one another in a reliable and predictable way.

In the context of modeling, patterns are any aspects of the exemplar's beliefs, thoughts, feelings, and behaviors that are consistent to the point of being predictable. These patterns reveal themselves as we contrast and compare examples of the exemplar manifesting her ability. We are looking for what is the *same* in all of the examples in terms of beliefs, behaviors, and so on. A pattern is whatever shows up as a consistent and predictable element in the exemplar's structure of experience.

How many examples do you need in order to be confident that you have identified a pattern? One example is not enough. With just one example you have no way of knowing what is peculiar to the particular situation of that example and what is characteristic of the *ability* regardless of the peculiarities of the situation. For instance, suppose our exemplar for forgiveness describes an incident in which she forgave someone who cut her off in traffic, explaining, "I recalled having done the same myself once," and "I saw the humor in the situation." There are no patterns revealed in this; there is only description. We need a second example. When she describes a second example of forgiving a friend who had betrayed her, we find that the exemplar saw *no* humor in the situation. But she *did* "recall having done the same myself once." This shows us that "finding humor in the situation" is not a pattern, but that "recalling having done the same myself" *is* likely to be a pattern. To confirm that it is in fact a pattern, and not simply a coincidence, it is a good idea to explore a third example.

Capturing Description

As we have seen, different questions will organize our experiences in different ways. The significance of this effect extends beyond simply reminding us to be aware of how we phrase our questions during elicitation. The larger lesson here is that words carry meaning from one person to another. It is primarily through the words and phrases that our exemplar uses that we gain access to the content and structure of her world.

In casual conversation, when someone says something in a way that does not fit with our own experience, we often re-interpret what has been said in our own words: "The way I would say that is…" But as we know, how you say something can matter very much in terms of where it leads your experience: words carry experience. Because the experience that we are after in modeling is that of the exemplar, it is important to use *her* words in capturing descriptions of her internal process. Of course, your exemplar may use a word whose meaning is new to you, or is unclear, or is obviously being used in a way that is different from how you would use it. In any of these cases, rather than substituting your own words (and, so, the experiences that go with them), it is much better to ask your exemplar for the examples and explanations you need in order to understand them in their own terms.

Necessary and Sufficient

To watch Fred Astaire dance is to watch the essence of dance. He dazzles us with movement, revealing what is possible *in* moving. The reason we can see and feel in Astaire what dance *is,* is because his movements are not obscured by excess. Every movement is all that is needed to express that moment…and to flow into the next movement. It is elegance in action.

We want our models to dance elegantly, like Astaire, carrying us into the ability with those movements of our experience that are just what is needed—no more, no less. Elegance is the quality of using only what is *necessary and sufficient* to get the desired effect. The effect we are after here is to manifest the ability we are modeling. Keep in mind that:

> *A model is not intended to supply everything;*
> *a model is intended to make everything possible.*

A model that requires us to adopt only one pattern to manifest a certain ability is no more elegant than the model of a different ability that requires us to manifest two dozen patterns. In each case it takes what it takes; the idea of elegance is that the model not include *more* than it takes.

But are not all the details and nuances of experience important for true competence in an ability? Yes, they are. But true competence—and the details and nuances that make that possible—come in the use of the ability. Adopting the structure of the ability starts a snowball of new awareness that picks up more and more relevant details as it rolls down the hill of experience. You may have had an example of this when you learned to play a sport (or to drive a car, meditate, play an instrument, paint, or dance). In learning to play tennis, for instance, you were taught how to grip and swing the racquet in order to hit the ball well. But it was using that strategy that put you in a position to quickly learn how to adjust your body to meet the many different ways in which the ball can come at you, so that your swing consistently hits the ball into your opponent's court. *The structure offered by the model will act as a filter on your experience, allowing you to notice and respond to things that previously were transparent to you.*

Even if it is not necessary to include everything, is it still a good idea to make the model as rich and detailed as possible? Aside from the daunting fact that including everything in the model will make the gathering of information a monumental task, it may also get in the way of your actually being able to take on the model.

Models are not crammed into people; models are *accommodated* by people. The more room there is in the model for you to find yourself, the more readily you will be able to adopt it. Rearranging a few pieces of furniture in your house to make it comfortable is one thing. But if making your house comfortable means taking out walls, raising the ceilings, replacing the windows, repainting... that is quite a different enterprise, and not so easily done. The more a model simply offers that which is necessary and sufficient, the more room it leaves for you to easily connect with it. In order to understand this idea more clearly, we can draw an analogy between the detail of models and the range of iconographic imagery in cartoons. (Figure 4)

Of the five images in Scott McCloud's illustration, the photographic image on the left is obviously the most complete and realistic representation. But is it the one we can most easily identify with? That photographic image is so clearly and fully who *that* person is that there is little room in it for us to find ourselves. As the images progressively lose the details of a particular (male) person, they reveal more and more of what is essential to "personhood," and it becomes easier for us to identify with the image. There is, in a sense, more *room* for us to find ourselves in the image.

Of course, eliminating detail can go too far, as well. The last image in

from *Understanding Comics* © 1993 Scott McCloud (used with permission)

Figure 4

McCloud's illustration has lost so much detail that it has no character or quality other than "face." Yes, now everyone can identify with it, but there is almost no information in it, and so it does not take us anywhere. In our modeling we are after a middle ground. That middle ground is found by capturing those patterns of the exemplar's experience necessary and sufficient to *manifest* her ability in ourselves.

THE ELICITATION PROTOCOL

As we said, we will be giving you specific elicitation questions that generally work well to help your exemplar access the information you need. We have also found that there is a particular elicitation sequence that, if used, makes the process smoother, more efficient, and more effective. The following Elicitation Protocol describes that sequence. This is the same protocol used in the accompanying DVD.

As you will see, the Elicitation Protocol refers to distinctions in the Array—such as *Criterion*—that we have not yet discussed (though you may recall them from the DVD). We will describe these modeling distinctions in detail in the following chapters. For the moment, however, we simply want to get a sense of the overall flow of the process of elicitation; you can return to it with deeper understanding after reading the following chapters and reviewing the DVD :

Modeling Elicitation Protocol

---

1. Ask your exemplar to define the ability.

> This helps orient her to the particular class of experiences from which you want her to draw examples.

2. Have your exemplar identify three examples of manifesting her ability.

> Identifying the examples before you begin the elicitation is useful in a couple of ways. Often an exemplar will really want to search for "good" examples. Taking care of this up front will allow your exemplar to easily move from one example to another, rather than interrupting the flow of the elicitation with looking for another "good" example.

> Establishing the examples now also gives you the opportunity to make sure that they are examples of just what you want to model. If one or some are not, you can clarify what are good examples, and help your exemplar find them.

3. Pick one of the examples to serve as the *home* example. Then ask your exemplar to: "Tell me about [that example] as an example of [the ability]."

> Have your exemplar select (or do it yourself) one of the examples of her manifesting the Ability as being a particularly meaningful and rich one. This example will then serve as the *home example*, which is the example from which you will *first* gather information.

> Asking your exemplar to, "Tell me about [that example] as an example of [the ability]," is an opportunity for your exemplar to tell her story of her ability. This is something exemplars expect to be asked to do and, so, a relief for them when they get to do it. It also gives you an opportunity to get a sense of the territory you will be exploring with your exemplar, which can help you keep oriented when you are later focusing on specific elements of her experience.

4. Identify the Criterion operating in the home example.

Though you can begin anywhere in the Array, it is almost always best to start with the Criterion. Because everything in the Array—and, so, the ability—happens in relation to the Criterion, it will give you and your exemplar a reference point to judge the relevance of the information you gather as you move through the elicitation.

5. Go to the other two examples to find the Criterion operating in them. Compare the Criterion in each of those examples with the one you found in the home example in order to confirm—and possibly refine—the Criterion for the ability.

This will quickly either confirm that you have identified the correct Criterion or, if not, reveal what the Criterion actually is as you and your exemplar look for patterns across the examples.

6. Elicit the rest of the Belief Template—Definition, Evidence, Enabling and Motivating Cause-Effects—in this same way (that is, identify that element of the exemplar's experience first in the home example, then confirm—and refine—what you find by comparing it with your exemplar's experience in the other examples).

You will find that your exemplar quickly comes to understand the comparisons you are making, and will start searching for the patterns in her experience across examples even before you ask for them. This, plus your exemplar being able to see your notes (on a chart, board, or paper, as we suggested earlier), will turn your exemplar into your collaborator.

7. Elicit the Primary and Secondary Strategies in the home example. Then confirm—and refine—them by comparing them with your exemplar's strategies in the other examples.

8. Elicit the Sustaining Emotion in the home example. Then confirm— and refine—it by comparing it with your exemplar's emotion in the other examples.

9. Elicit the External Behavior in the home example. Then confirm— and refine—them by comparing them with your exemplar's behaviors in the other examples.

Elicitation is not the end of the modeling process. Once you have done your initial information gathering, you will be creating the model, weeding out what is not essential to the ability, and putting what remains into a form that makes it accessible. Part of this process of refining the model may include going back to your exemplar to get certain things clarified. For that reason we suggest that, after finishing the elicitation, you ask your exemplar to give you a little more of her time in the future to review the model with her. (We have never had an exemplar refuse to do this. In fact, they are almost always very eager to learn what you have discovered about them.)

The next step in the process is to work with the model to acquire it; that is, to make its various patterns of experience real in your *own* experience. (Examples of reviewing, refining, and acquiring a model are on the DVD, and we will cover these topics in detail in Chapters 12, 13, and 14.)

Even then the process of modeling is not over. Once you have a model that is working in you in imagination, it is time to test it in the real world. Actually manifesting the ability in the real world will give you experiences that may lead to further refinements of the model, refinements that make the model even more effective for you.

Now we step from overview to action. In the next eight chapters we will take each of the elements of experience in turn and explore how they function, as well as the details of their elicitation. Throughout that exploration we will be drawing upon the elicitation presented on the accompanying DVD to enrich our understanding of these elements of experience. After that we will cover how to organize the information you have gathered into an Experiential Array, and how to then use it to acquire the Ability. But before an Ability can be acquired, we must first model its structure. We begin with the structure of beliefs.

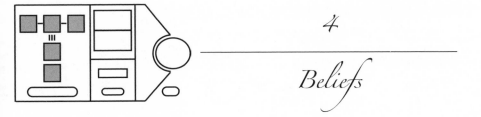

4

Beliefs

The notion of "beliefs" covers a lot of experiential ground. People believe that God exists, that God does not exist, that a person ought to look out for oneself first, that a person ought to give of oneself to others, that conservatives are right, that liberals are right, that control is imperative, that freedom is imperative. People believe that the world is round, that we never went to the moon, that whales and redwoods must be preserved, that if you drop a glass it is likely to break, and that Elvis is still alive. People have beliefs about who they are, about how the world works, about what is true, not true, possible, and impossible. The range of beliefs is as wide as human experience itself.

Beliefs influence virtually everything we do. A moment's reflection upon the subtle, swift, and often unconscious background to any one of your daily choices and responses will reveal the pervasive power of beliefs. For example:

> Walking down the street, you finish a candy bar and, believing ***people should be respectful of the environment***, you toss the wrapper into a trash can. Then you spot someone else casually dropping their candy wrapper on the sidewalk! You are suddenly flooded with disgust that someone could be so disrespectful.

> You are trying to get that report done, but not getting very far. Wondering why it is so difficult this time, you remember that ***"I always seem to do my best work when I have Afro-Cuban music playing."*** So you put some on.

> A friend calls to ask you to help him move next weekend. You had planned to go skiing. Nevertheless, you agree to help him. After all, ***friends help friends***.

Each of us can multiply these examples a thousand-fold. And in every case the pattern is the same: Your response to the situation is significantly influenced by the beliefs you are holding in that situation.

Because of the fundamental and pervasive influence of beliefs upon our thoughts, feelings, and actions, they are an essential distinction in the modeling of human abilities. In almost every example of a human ability that we might want to model, *underlying beliefs* play a significant and necessary role.

UNDERLYING BELIEFS

Whether we are aware of it or not, we are always expressing our beliefs. These expressions may come as words, as when a teacher asserts, "You have to challenge your students so they can eventually discover that they can master anything." Beliefs will also be expressed through actions, as when that same teacher gives her students a book that she knows will be difficult to read (assigning it *because* "you have to challenge your students so they can eventually discover that they can master anything").

The richness of language (and of behavior as well) makes it possible for us to express a particular belief in endless ways. As an example, consider the following beliefs:

"Hard work provides a good foundation."
"I need to get busy on that project if it is to get anywhere."
"You get out only what you put in."
"Without effort there is no accomplishment."
"He will never amount to anything until he breaks a sweat at something."
"Choosing between brains and diligence, I'll take diligence every time."

Although each of these statements is manifestly different from any of the others, they are all expressions of the same underlying belief that "effort is required in order to attain goals." An excellent example of this redundancy in the expression of beliefs can be found in an interview with Artie Shaw, a legendary jazz clarinetist and leader of the famous Artie Shaw Orchestra:

> The main thing was to get rid of non-essentials. Basically when you're hearing a piece of music there's the melody and the rhythm pulse behind it. It could be a piano...it could be a piano, bass guitar, and drums, whatever. But there's a pulse and a melody. Now anything you add to that has got to be done very carefully, because you are taking away from the attention of the

average lay listener, who is interested in the melody and in the beat, if he's dancing. When you make an arrangement, as I put it, make it as simple as you can. If there's too much in there that doesn't belong, get rid of it. My job as a leader was to take the music that was brought to me... these were accomplished musicians but they would forget that the audience wasn't an accomplished musician. They didn't know what was going on. My job was to try to act as intermediary between their complex notions and ideas about the tune and what the audience wanted. And I tried my best to keep it musically as good and exciting and valid as I could and at the same time cut out the irrelevancies.[1]

In this extract, Shaw pronounces, explains, recommends, recalls, justifies, and judges. He says many things; consider whether or not these many things express *different* beliefs:

"The main thing was to get rid of non-essentials."

"When you make an arrangement, as I put it, make it as simple as you can."

"If there's too much in there that doesn't belong, get rid of it."

"Now anything you add to that has got to be done very carefully, because you are taking away from the attention of the average lay listener, who is interested in the melody and in the beat, if he's dancing."

"Cut out the irrelevancies."

These are obviously different statements. When we look below the *surface* of what he is saying, however, we discover that they all spring from the same underlying belief: "It's important to get rid of non-essentials."

If we were modeling Artie Shaw's ability to arrange compositions for a jazz band, we would not want to include in our model all the ways he has of expressing his fundamental idea that "it's important to get rid of non-essentials." Those infinite forms of expression constitute an ocean that can never be drained. It is much easier to grasp the underlying belief that gives rise to those endless expressions. We can then use that underlying belief to generate in ourselves the same *kinds* of perceptions and choices that it generated in Artie Shaw.

As the interview with Shaw—and any conversation—reveals, masses of

---

[1] From "The Mystery of Artie Shaw," segment: "Will the Beguine Ever End?" Interviewed and produced by Ted Hallock, KBOO, Portland, Oregon. (Used with permission.)

beliefs are always being expressed. How are we to make our way through this vast and endlessly diverse territory, and identify the underlying beliefs? Fortunately, our exploration is made easier for us by the fact that there are just two patterns that form the structure of all beliefs: Equivalences and Cause-Effects.

EQUIVALENCES

Many of our beliefs are expressions of the meaningful connections we have made between two or more experiences. For instance, in her memoir, *An American Childhood*, Annie Dillard describes a trip with her mother to a branch of the Carnegie Library in Pittsburgh. It was the early 1950s, and the library was in Homewood, "a Negro section of town." Getting out of the car, they encountered Henry Watson, the beau of the Dillard family's maid, walking with some other men:

> It would embarrass him, I thought, if I said hello to him in front of his friends. I was wrong. He spied me, picked me up—books and all—swung me as he always did, and introduced Mother and me to his friends. Later, as we were climbing the long stone steps to the library's door, Mother said, "That's what I mean by good manners." (p.80)

Dillard's mother made a meaningful connection ("this means that") for her daughter between Henry Watson's behavior and "good manners"; she was establishing an *equivalence* between the two.

As newborns we were awash in undifferentiated experience. Then, over time, our world was marked out and equivalences were made for us. There were objects (mommy, daddy, cow, building, Christmas present, George, spinach), qualities (red, rough, soft, loud, sour, fresh), relationships (too much, enough, closed, above, inside), behaviors (running, thinking, whining, squirming, babbling, smiling), personality characteristics (smart, inconsiderate, lady-like, gentlemanly, happy, polite,) and abstractions (mind, democracy, ideals, good, bad, relativity), and so on. The world of our perceptual experience was soon filled with equivalences.

Equivalences are not passive observations, but active agents of experience. Once established, an equivalence acts as a filter on your experience. That is, from the moment an equivalence is acquired (or changed), it becomes the basis for making meaning out of your perceptions and experiences in particular situations. For instance, a colleague of ours never thought of himself as a courageous person. Indeed, because he often felt afraid he thought of himself as something of a coward. Once we pointed out to him that being courageous was not about being fearless, but about forging ahead *despite* feeling fear, he suddenly recognized that, in fact, he often *is* courageous; his equivalence for "courageous" had changed. Not only did he start seeing himself in a different light, but because he now saw that "I am a courageous person," he began to throw himself into situations that he previously avoided.

CAUSE-EFFECTS

In addition to equivalences, our beliefs can also be expressions of the causal connections we establish when we perceive that *something* consistently and predictably leads to *something else*. These connections are called *cause-effects*. While the connection in equivalences is one of "this means that," the connection in cause-effects is one of "this *causes* that." For instance, you might notice that regular exercise causes you to have more energy; or that when you work hard you succeed; or that when you believe in yourself the world offers you opportunities. With enough consistent examples of a particular cause-effect relationship, it becomes real to you and takes its place as one of your beliefs about how the world works.

As with equivalences, once a cause-effect is established it operates as a filter on your experience, guiding both your perceptions and actions. Suppose, for example, you had some experiences in which you treated others well and they, in turn, treated you well. From this you might come to believe the cause-effect, "If you treat people well, they will treat you well." If you hold that belief, you will think about how to treat people well, try to treat people well, and notice when you are and are not treating people well.

Unstated Connections

You can probably think of examples of beliefs that do not appear to fit either the Equivalence or Cause-Effect patterns; for instance, "I believe Frank is a reliable person," and "I believe the sun will rise tomorrow." However, for this person to believe that "Frank is a reliable person," she must have an equivalence for what a "reliable person" *is*. As it happens, Frank *fits* that description. She is simply not stating the underlying equivalence. If she did, she might say something like "Frank is a reliable person, which means that he always follows through on what he says he will do."

Similarly, underling the belief that "the sun will rise tomorrow" is an unstated cause-effect. If stated it might go something like, "The sun will rise tomorrow because the world keeps turning."

We often leave our Equivalences and Cause-Effects unstated because we assume—usually correctly—that there is no need to be explicit about them. Only a cranky epistemologist would greet "the sun will rise tomorrow" with a demand for an explanation of how you know that it will; the rest of us know what is behind such a belief. Likewise, we often assume that others share our Equivalences, so it does not occur to us to explain what we mean when we say that "Frank is reliable." (If that Equivalence is not shared, however—for instance, the other person believes that "reliable" means "the person does whatever I want him to do"—misunderstanding is inevitable.)

All beliefs, then, are built upon the two patterns of Equivalence and Cause-Effect. They may not be explicitly expressed in what the person is saying. Nevertheless, they are there, organizing our experiences and behavior along certain lines.

The "Belief Template"

The distinctions of Equivalence and Cause-Effect make it easier to simplify the exemplar's masses of expressed beliefs by helping us pinpoint the few *underlying* beliefs that give rise to all of those expressions. This still leaves us with a question regarding *which* of those underlying Equivalences and Cause-Effects are important to identify if we want to model our exemplar.

Through our modeling work we have identified those classes of Equivalences and Cause-Effects that are essential to a useful model of any ability. These essential Equivalences and Cause-Effects are captured in the Belief Template, a graphic model operating *inside* the Experiential Array. (Figure 5)

As you can see, one of the advantages of the Belief Template is that it shows us how the essential Equivalences and Cause-Effects (the exemplar's beliefs) relate to one another. After all, our beliefs do not operate independently. They work together to form the subjective world through which we perceive and act.

In the next two chapters we will take you through the Belief Template, describing in detail each of the essential distinctions it captures.

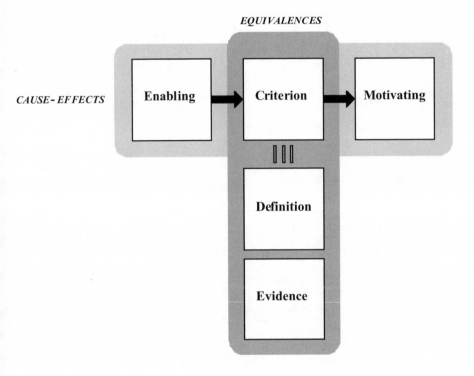

Figure 5

5

Beliefs: Equivalences

The world is absolutely full of objects, events, qualities, and experiences. For the most part, these "things" have no intrinsic meaning or significance. We can *give* them meaning, however. For example, perhaps in your eyes having a red sports car might mean you are a racy kind of person, while in someone else's eyes it might mean that you are a success. Or a friend who frequently touches your arm and asks probing questions might mean to you that she is a warm person, while to someone else your friend's behavior means she is an intrusive person. Making these kinds of connections between things (objects, events, qualities, experiences)—the process of creating *equivalences*—is one of the ways we make meaning. When an equivalence (meaning) relationship also becomes significant—that is, it becomes something that is really important to us—we have established a *Criterion*.

Criteria

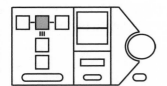

Composer Igor Stravinsky was commissioned by the Venice Festival to write an original work. His contribution turned out to be fifteen minutes long. The officials of the festival complained to Stravinsky that this was too short. "Well, then," Stravinsky replied calmly, "play it again."

All of us periodically face situations that require difficult choices: whether to move to another city, buy a house, have a child, get married, separate from a partner, or change profession. Often it is in the process of making such demanding decisions that we become aware of what is important to us. Once we know what is truly important, the choice to make becomes clear (even if it is still not easy to accept).

As we know, different people facing the need to make the same decision will often make different choices. They make different choices because they have different ideas about what is important. When buying a home, for instance, one person may be focused on spaciousness, someone else on convenience, and others on low maintenance, or proximity to good schools, or affordability. These are examples of the various *criteria* people use when choosing a home. Typical criteria people bring to the decision about whether or not to have children include emotional readiness, job security, time for care-giving, and expense. In deciding on a change in profession, criteria might include financial security, personal development, excitement, and independence. In each of these contexts, the criteria are serving as—and being applied as—standards of evaluation.

Though not always as obvious as when making a life-changing decision, this same process of evaluating with respect to criteria is operating in virtually everything we do. For example, ask yourself "What is important to me as I read these pages?" It may not have occurred to you that something *is* important to you until you asked the question. But when you ask yourself that question, you will find that there are *particular* things you are evaluating as you read. Perhaps you want to "understand" the concepts presented here. Or perhaps as you read your attention is focused on the "usefulness" of the material, or its "clarity," or its "originality." It may instead be that what is important to you as you read is having "fun," finding keys to "personal power," discovering "new possibilities," "freedom," or any of a thousand other human concerns. The significance of criteria is that they guide what we attend to and to what we respond. Movie director John Waters gives a delightful example of the effect of criteria:

> There's no such thing as a bad movie if you go to a movie watching detail only. If you really hate the movie, look at the lamps. The movie is about lamps, and then it's never boring. It's always surprising and exciting.[1]

Criteria act as filters on our experience in much the same way as colored lenses filter light. The world is awash in the full spectrum of sunlight, but if you are wearing red goggles the only light that is transmitted to you will be shades of red. Similarly, reading these pages while holding the criterion of "usefulness" is like wearing a pair of "usefulness" goggles. As you read *through* those goggles you will particularly notice references to how to use or apply the concepts. Your "usefulness" goggles will also probably have you generating your own ideas about when, where, and how the concepts can be useful. In other words, you will be reading *for* "usefulness." However,

---

[1] From an interview on National Public Radio's, "Fresh Air," February 5, 2004.

someone who reads these same pages wearing the criterion goggles of "clarity" may not notice the many opportunities for "useful" applications that you discovered. That person will instead be occupied with noticing how well things are being explained, how well the various points hang together, and perhaps generating possibilities for clearer explanations.

Of course, we can evaluate several criteria at the same time. However, when we elicit criteria from an exemplar we usually find that she has one criterion *in focus*. Like everyone else, she will have many criteria operating at the same time, but one of these will be in focus; that is, her attention is guided by one particular criterion. This is not surprising. We all know from personal experience that trying to *simultaneously* satisfy several different criteria can lead to confusion, conflict, and lack of effectiveness. Part of what makes exemplars effective at what they do is that they have one criterion organizing and guiding their thinking and behavior when they are manifesting their Ability. In the Belief Template, then:

> The Criterion is *the primary standard of evaluation*
> *the exemplar uses when manifesting the Ability.*[2]

In one of our modeling seminars we enjoyed a simple and dramatic example of the essential importance of a Criterion in manifesting an Ability. Derek wanted to learn to take good photographs. From his photographer exemplar he discovered that the first step (a sub-ability) is "recognizing a possible picture to take." When he modeled this sub-ability he learned that his exemplar is always looking for and responding to "contrast" (the Criterion), by which she meant any adjacent and marked difference in brightness, color, shape, texture, size, and content. After offering the group *only* this Criterion, everyone suddenly started looking around the room and *seeing possible pictures*. The shadows cast by the chair upon the floor, the red shirt meeting the blue slacks, the curve of the potted plant against the rectangles of the window panes, the smooth hand upon the corduroy, the old man walking by holding the hand of a child...all these instances of "contrast" now jumped out at us as possible subjects for photographs.

---

[2] Arrays containing the definitions and elicitation questions for all of the elements of an Array will be found in the Appendices.

Elicitation Questions for the Criterion

"When you are [ability], what is important to you?"
— or —
"When you are [ability], what are you evaluating?"

For most of the elements of the Array we will offer you two questions. Both versions seek the same information, but use different phrasing. If one question does not help your exemplar access the information, switching to the other question will usually be effective. The [brackets] describe the content to insert into the question. For example, if you are modeling the ability to appreciate abstract art, you would ask, "When you are appreciating abstract art, what is important to you?"

EXAMPLES

Throughout the rest of the book, whenever we introduce the elicitation questions for an element of the Experiential Array we will use Adam, Bridgit, and Claire as our exemplars. As a professional event organizer, Adam has the ability to plan celebrations that people really enjoy. Bridgit is an elementary school teacher who has the ability to be patient with her students. And Claire is good at designing web sites that people find easy to use.

Q: When you are planning a celebration, what is important to you?

Adam: What I really want is that *everyone is included* in whatever is going on.

Q: When you are being patient with a child as she is learning something, what are you evaluating?

Bridgit: Is there *movement*. I don't care about the end point, really, only that she is moving in that direction.

Q: When you are designing the user interface for a web site, what is important to you?

Claire: I want it to be *elegant*. An interface that has *elegance* is just... well, it's just so great when they are.

As you can see, the Criterion is typically expressed by one word, or by a short phrase. We will talk about the reason for this in the next section. For now it is only important to recognize that this economy of words is typical of the Criterion, and that you are looking for that one word or phrase that "names" your exemplar's primary focus of attention when she is manifesting her Ability.

"Being Passionate About Something" – Eliciting the Criterion

Throughout the rest of the book we will be drawing our primary examples of Array elicitation from the accompanying DVD demonstration of modeling Kendall's ability to be passionate about something. We began the elicitation of Kendall's Array by identifying her Criterion in her *home example* of being passionate about her work:

> David: Going back to that time yesterday when you were doing the teleclass, as you are *there*, working with these people on the phone, what's important to you?

> Kendall: What's important to me is that they're getting what they want. That what I'm delivering is *useful* to them, that it's *helpful* to them.

Kendall's first response is "they're getting what they want." But this is immediately followed by a further clarification, that it is "useful" and "helpful." The fact that these two expressions specify some of the kinds of things that her clients could "want" suggests that they are criteria. In addition, her voice tonality and facial expressions mark out "useful" and "helpful" as being really true for her.

By having her then compare her experience of "useful" and "helpful," she then resolves the distinction between the two, explaining that "Helpful has more of an element of caring." We ultimately find out that what is really important to her *in the context of her work* is to be "helpful." We do not yet know if that is her Criterion when being *passionate* in general, however. To do that, we need to compare it with her other examples of being passionate:

> David: So in relation to your husband and your relationship, being in love with him, when you are in that context, in that situation where you are getting to manifest and experience that passion, What's important to you then?

Kendall: I actually want him to know how wonderful I think he is, and I want him to know how much I love him.

David: Why?

Kendall: Because it feels really good. It feels really good for me. I just love that, I love telling somebody that I love them, and this ties into it in lots of different ways, like leaving little notes or phone calls, *being appreciative* for the things he does, which is a lot.

Kendall does not mention being "helpful" here. Instead, what jumps out here is "being appreciative." Since her work and her relationship are both contexts in which she is passionate, the Criterion must be similar or the same in both, so we compare the two examples. Recalling that it was very important to Kendall that her clients appreciate how helpful something was for them, we ask about the importance of "being appreciative" in the context of her work. She confirms that it is very important. Checking the third example:

David: In the context of being with your horses – and that may not be actually with them, perhaps, maybe it's even thinking about them, I don't know – but when you are in the context of being with your horses, what's important to you then?

Kendall: …What's important to me about riding…I want to say everything! What's important to me with riding…I love the feel of it…From the heart, what's important is loving every moment of it. And when I'm working with my horse, whether it's grooming him or tacking up, riding or training or cooling out or doing whatever. It's really *appreciating* and loving every moment of it. …So what's important to me is *appreciating* him and communicating with him the very best that I possibly can at any given moment.

She answers by describing some of what she appreciates; that is, in her response she is demonstrating that what she does is to be appreciative. Now her pattern is clear to her, as well, and she simply states, "So what's important to me is *appreciating*..." The Criterion, then, is "Being Appreciative."

Definition

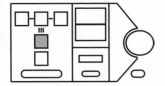

Happiness is when what you think, what you say, and what you do are in harmony.

– Mahatma Gandhi

When evaluating animal species according to whether or not they are "successful," most people will probably choose human beings as "the most successful" species. Our ability to manipulate our world through language, tools, and technology is unmatched by any other species. We are the obvious choice. But what about ants? After all, ants are far more numerous than human beings. Or how about crocodiles, which have survived basically unchanged for over 200 million years? Perhaps the accolade should fall upon the gray whales, who have learned to coexist with each other without war or cruelty?

What we consider the most successful species depends upon how we define "successful." If it means *able to manipulate the world through the use of language, tools, and technology*, then human beings are the most successful species. But to someone who defines "successful" as *having the greatest numbers*, then ants have us humans beat. If "successful" means *enduring throughout the millennia*, we humans are just getting started; our ability to last is relatively untested compared to that of the crocodile. If one considers as "successful" a species that *has transcended the willingness to kill its own kind,* human beings are not even in the running. Each of these is a different definition for the criterion, "successful."

We tend to assume that the words we use mean the same to everyone. Most of the time, that assumption works well enough. Still, there have been times when you and a friend have been as far apart on the meaning of a particular concept as a stock broker from New York and a Mbuti pygmy from the Ituri forest talking about "security." All of us have many examples in our personal histories of misunderstandings and arguments arising from unshared definitions for something important to us (that is, for a criterion). For instance, a husband and wife may have different ideas about what it means to "participate" in family life: For him it means "doing my share to support the family financially, keeping the house in good repair, and taking an interest in the kids"; for her it means "being involved in the daily decisions, needs, and difficulties of me, the kids, and 'us'." Sharing our criteria with someone means more than using the same word; we need to share the meaning inside the word, as well:

> The Definition is *a description of the kind of*
> *experience the Criterion means to this person.*

We have said that our exemplar's Criterion acts as the primary filter on her experience when she is manifesting her ability. Now we see that we do not really know what that filter is until we also have our exemplar's Definition of that Criterion.

For example, Derek discovered from his photographer exemplar that the Definition of "Contrast" is, "any adjacent and marked difference in brightness, color, shape, texture, size, and content." When it comes to taking pictures, for many of us the notion of "contrast" simply means differences in brightness. The exemplar's Definition, however, opens our eyes to a much wider notion of contrast. Without her Definition we could use the Criterion of "contrast" and still miss most of the potential pictures she sees—those of contrasting shapes, textures, contents, and so on.

The Definition is the exemplar's description of the kind of experience she is looking for when she is operating in the context of her ability. Consciously or unconsciously, she is evaluating, "Am I having *that* experience?" If she is, great; her way of operating in that context is working. If she is not having *that* experience, she changes her behavior and does something different until she *does* have *that* experience. The particular experience described in the Definition is what the exemplar wants to have; the Criterion is the label for that experience.

Why is it necessary to go to the trouble of identifying both the Criterion and its Definition? Why not elicit just the Definition, since that is the description of the experience that is orienting our exemplar's perceptions and behavior?

The usefulness of the Criterion lies precisely in the fact that it *is* a label for a set of experiences. Our colleague, Steve Andreas, aptly describes the Criterion as "the handle on the suitcase" of the experience. To use the label is to grab the whole of the experience, just as grabbing the suitcase handle necessarily brings with it the suitcase and all its contents. The Criterion is a simple way to refer to or access what may well be an extensive and detailed description of the exemplar's experience. It is also what your exemplar is most likely to use when referring to where she is putting her attention. However, if we want to be sure that we know what is in the suitcase of experience we have just grabbed with her Criterion handle, we need to look inside it; we need its Definition.

Elicitation Questions for the Definition

"What is [Criterion]?"

— or —

"What do you mean by [Criterion]?"

EXAMPLES

Q: What do you mean by "everyone is included"?

Adam: That *whatever is going on, each person has a role in it, or is somehow directly involved.*

Q: What do you mean by "movement"?

Bridgit: Well, I mean that *she can do something she couldn't do before, or understand something she didn't understand before. Even the tiniest of things is enough.*

Q: What is "elegance"?

Claire: A web site where the *things just flow easily from one point to another*, that's elegance.

The Definition is much like a dictionary definition, which is an abstraction or description that presents the nature or essential qualities of something. When asked to define a Criterion, exemplars often instead respond with *examples* of what the Criterion is, rather than the abstracted description of the *kinds* of experiences that the Criterion covers. (This is like asking someone what they usually carry in their suitcase and getting the answer "Well, I have a pair of red socks in there.") For instance, suppose that Adam did not answer with a Definition, but instead offered an example, such as "If there is a presentation to make—of an award or something—I try to make sure that everyone gets a chance to touch it or hold it, and is present when it's given. Even kitchen staff." Some celebrations do not include awards, however, so this *example of* including people probably does not define "Everyone is included."

If the exemplar gives you an example instead of a Definition, ask for additional examples. Then you can ask your exemplar, "What kind of experience are those examples all examples *of*?" For instance, suppose Adam came up with the additional example, "Well, at a company Halloween party I coordinated I made sure that the servers, people at the door—even the car valets—were all in costumes." By comparing these examples (and others, if necessary), Adam will probably recognize his pattern of getting every person at the event involved.

Alternatively, *you* can look for how the examples are all the same (the pattern that ties all the examples together). When you offer your version of the Definition to your exemplar, she will know right away if it fits her experience or not. Even if it does not fit, it will be useful to your exemplar; offering her what her experience is *not*, will almost always help her bring into focus what it actually *is*.

"Being Passionate About Something" – Eliciting the Definition

We have already identified that when Kendall is being passionate about something, her Criterion is "Being Appreciative":

David: Now, but I want to understand just what you mean by "appreciative," because I've got my idea about it, but I want to know what you mean by it.

Kendall: Okay.

David: So for you, what do you mean by "appreciative?"

Kendall: It is…it's feeling lucky, you know it's feeling really blessed and lucky and…Um, let me think…you know, I don't know if wanting just to share that—no, you know what it is, it's feeling blessed and lucky and at the same time it's *noticing*—because part of being appreciative for me is *really noticing what's going on, as best as I can tell, in the experience of the other person, or in the experience of my horse*.

[later]

…It's like when I think of working with this woman with her website, and she was saying something—her name is Debbie—and I said, "You know Debbie"—I don't remember what I said or what the topic was, but I just remember pointing out to her, "You know, Debbie, you're *really good* at this," and pointing that out to her and she said, "Oh, yeah, I didn't see it that way." And with my horse, pointing out to him, "You just did that *really* well."

David: So, "really" is a word that keeps coming up here—

Kendall: Yes.

David: —so, maybe it's noticing what others do that's really...

Kendall: *Special*. Yeah, it's noticing what they do that's special,
because they just don't see it.

Kendall's first answer is that it is "feeling blessed and lucky." We do not seize upon this as the Definition, first because *"Being* Appreciative" and her examples suggest *doing* something, rather than simply feeling a certain way. Second, we can see and hear that she is unsure about her initial answer. (She later confirms that feeling blessed and lucky is a "by-product" of being appreciative.) By contrast, her "really noticing what's going on, as best as I can tell, in the experience of the other person" tumbles out with congruence and confidence.

In the example that she gives of appreciating Debbie, Kendall includes telling her what she is appreciating. We want to check if that is also an essential part of what "Being Appreciative" means:

David: ...So, being appreciative is noticing the detailed things
that others do that are special.

Kendall: And the other can be an animal or a human being.

David: And is it "being appreciative" if you don't let
them know?

Kendall: No.

When we look back at all of the examples Kendall gave us of her being appreciative we find that the Definition, "noticing the detailed things that others do that are special, and telling them about it," describes them all.

Evidence

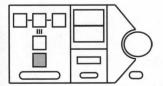

In the combative 60s, during an interview with rock musician Frank Zappa, talk show host Joe Pyne (who had a wooden leg) smugly said to Zappa, "I see you have long hair. You must be a girl." Zappa coolly replied, "I see you have a wooden leg. You must be a table."

One of the authors called in a plumber to fix the bathtub, which was taking 20 minutes to empty. The plumber filled the tub with water and opened the drain. The usual gurgling began as the water trickled down the drain, and after a few seconds the plumber announced, "It seems to be working just fine." When the author pointed out that the water level in the tub was hardly dropping, the plumber explained, "Listen…you hear that sound the drain is making? That's what it sounds like when it's draining properly." He was not kidding. He knew that the drain was working; he had the *evidence* of the sound to prove it.

Though we are not always conscious of it, we have evidence for almost everything that is of importance to us. A person who cares about "honesty" will notice certain things about eye contact, facial symmetry, and voice tonality that indicate whether or not someone is being honest. People who value being "centered" typically have a particular feeling state that indicates to them when they *are* centered; the less they feel that state, the less centered they consider themselves to be. An executive may need the evidence of being the head of his own company to know that he is a "success," or receive testimonies of respect from his peers, or earn a particular level of income—or all of these bits of evidence. By contrast, a school teacher might know that she is a "success" when she sees even small improvements in her students over the course of a school year:

> Evidence is *what must be seen, heard, and/or*
> *felt, to know that the Criterion is being met.*[3]

Unlike the Criterion and its Definition, which tend to be abstractions, Evidence is described in terms of sensory experience. Associated with each of your Criteria are particular visual, auditory, and kinesthetic experiences that—for you—constitute the Evidence that your Criterion is satisfied (met, fulfilled, there, happening).

Evidence is not limited to what we see, hear, and feel with our senses, however. We can also have internally generated representations of all of these same sensory experiences. In addition to actually seeing a loved one, hearing her speak to you, feeling her hand in yours, and smelling her scent, you can also imagine seeing her delight, imagine hearing her gasp, and imagine feeling the hug she will give you when you tell her some good news. Internally generated experiences can serve as Evidence that is as meaningful

---

[3] For the sake of simplicity, we usually leave out "taste" and "smell" when talking about the sensory systems. But of course they are there, and may be essential Evidence for some Criteria (such as those you might encounter when modeling cooking abilities, or the ability to create a perfume).

and compelling as anything you perceive through your senses, and for some abilities internal evidence will be essential.

Evidence for a particular Criterion can be different for different people and, as with the Criterion and its Definition, these differences can significantly affect our experience and behavior. For instance, when we have asked people how they know they are in rapport with another person, the Evidence they usually describe is something like, "the person is making eye contact, leaning forward, and freely expressing himself," or "I feel an energetic connection between the two of us," or some combination of these kinds of perceptions. However, we know of a manager whose Evidence for being in rapport is not at all typical. She is in rapport when "I feel centered and sure about where I am and what's important to me." With this as her Evidence it is not surprising that her co-workers often feel that they have no rapport with her. Her Evidence puts her attention exclusively on *her* experience ("I feel centered, sure about where *I* am, what's important to *me*"), which is not well suited to evaluating what is typically thought of as rapport.

Threshold

We have been talking about Evidence as though it is always a yes/no proposition. Sometimes it is. But the richness and complexity of human experience is not always reducible to such clearly defined Evidence. Often a Criterion is satisfied by a *range* of evidence. When that is the case, it is only necessary for some of the Evidence to be experienced to cross a *threshold* that says, okay, the Criterion is satisfied.

In some cases the range of Evidence may be in the form of a continuum of experience. For instance, the person for whom being "centered" is important might have as her Evidence "feeling still inside, along the center of my body," *and* she evaluates her feeling of stillness along a continuum of experience. As long as she is "still" *enough* to cross some personal threshold, she will consider herself centered (and perhaps the more still she feels, the more centered she will consider herself to be).

Another possibility is that the range of Evidence is in the form of a set of experiences, and experiencing any one or some of the pieces of evidence in the set is enough to cross the threshold. If this were the case for the example of rapport we talked about above, we might consider that we are in rapport with someone if he is merely "making eye contact" with us, even though he is *not* leaning forward, and *not* freely expressing himself"; experiencing just *some* of the Evidence is enough in this case. (If he is *also* sitting forward and expressing himself freely, we would probably think we are *very much in rapport*.)

Specificity

No matter what your exemplar describes as her Evidence, it can always be made more and more specific. For instance, suppose our exemplar knows she is attractive to others when "They look at me with a certain expression." There are a lot of facial expressions; which one is that "certain expression?" When we ask our exemplar to specify the expression, she explains, "I can see that they are enjoying me." But how does she know that they are enjoying her? "The other person is smiling at me." We can keep going, having her be more specific about "smiling" ("The corners of the person's mouth are pulled back toward his ears, I can see at least some of his teeth, and wrinkles appear in the corner of his eyes"). When is Evidence sufficiently specified?

The answer is, *When you can do what your exemplar does*. Evidence needs to be described at the level of specificity that allows you to put your attention on the same sensory experiences your exemplar uses to know when her Criterion is satisfied. The description "They look at me with a certain expression," tells you almost nothing about what to attend to as Evidence. "I can see that the other person is enjoying being with me," is more specific, but still may not be enough for you know just what to attend to. "Smiling" may be enough of a description for you to be able to use it as Evidence, but "the corners of the person's mouth are pulled back toward his ears, etc." is probably more than you need to reproduce this exemplar's Ability.

Elicitation Questions for the Evidence

**"What do you see, hear and/or feel that lets
you know there is* [Criterion]?"**

*(or "you are" "it is" "you have" etc.)

EXAMPLES

Q: What do you see, hear and/or feel that lets you know that "everyone is included"?

Adam: Well, *no one is by themselves, and the groups of people are always changing. People feel free to ask for what they want, or even complain, and when there are group things, there is kind of one sound in the room, not quiet over here, laughing there, talking there,* and so on.

Q: What do you see, hear and/or feel that lets you know that there is "movement"?

Bridgit: You can see it in the child's face, really. *She's intent on what she's doing, and looks proud. Sometimes smiling.*

Q: What do you see, hear and/or feel that lets you know that an interface is "elegant"?

Claire: *You're not even thinking about how to find something; you just go to it. In fact, the best is when you aren't even aware that you are jumping from one place to another.*

Like the Definition, asking for the Evidence often elicits specific examples, rather than a description of what the exemplar *generally* sees, hears or feels that indicates that her Criterion is being satisfied. As with the Definition, ask for additional examples. Either your exemplar will be able to use her examples to pull the description together, or you can abstract the Evidence from the examples yourself and then offer it to her for confirmation and refinement.

"Being Passionate About Something" – Eliciting the Evidence

We know that it is important to Kendall to "Be Appreciative," and that this means "noticing the detailed things that others do that are special, and telling them about it." Now:

David: How do you know when you are being appreciative, that is, what is it you see, hear or feel that lets you know that you are noticing the detailed things that are special and that you're telling them about it?

Kendall: It's quite a lot of feeling, actually, and *I feel filled up inside, in my upper body and I have a sense of coming forward*—I don't know that I could really appreciate something if I was slouching and leaning back…I can't imagine doing that—so it feels somehow the energy feels very forward and my body feels filled up...*and I feel an eagerness inside*, as opposed to a calmness—it doesn't actually feel very calm—it feels eager and excited, *and I want to tell them something*. And sometimes I have to stop myself from interrupting them. So, the feeling's out, but then I want to say something. And I don't always *tell* them. In a work relationship, for example, it isn't always the right thing for me to *say* to them something, to make a statement. It's actually, I think, more useful if I ask a question so they discover it themselves.

David: But you know where you're taking them.

Kendall: Oh, absolutely. Yeah. And then I—except for the flowers, because they can't necessarily answer back (I never thought of it that way)—but with another human...how do I know I'm being appreciative?...I'm just trying on whether it's important that they *respond*, or not. Respond in a positive way...Actually it is. It is important.

David: Now, what constitutes a positive response? In other words, do they have to say something, like Debbie did, in your example—

Kendall: Right.

David: "Oh, you know—"

Kendall: *They have to brighten somehow.* They either have to say something or have a look on their face...I'm thinking of clients, my horse, my husband...*they have to have some verbal or non-verbal...lift to them.*

David: Evidence of some lift—

Kendall: I mean, if they just go along like nothing happens, then it's like, Hey! It doesn't quite cut it.

Kendall realizes that an important piece of Evidence for her is that others "respond in a positive way." This is a good example of an answer that requires further specification. When we try to put ourselves in her shoes, looking for a "positive response," we recognize that it could be almost anything, and that we do not yet know what to attend to. She explains that the person needs to "brighten somehow," that there is a "lift." We have a pretty good idea of what people look like when they "brighten." The "lift" is not so obvious, so we ask for more specification:

> David: "Lift." And this lift could be—
>
> Kendall: Just in their eyes.
>
> David: —actually physically, it could be in their facial expression, maybe in their voice tonality—
>
> Kendall: Right.
>
> David: —or they would be very explicit about the lift, saying, "You know, I feel so much better."
>
> Kendall: Right. They don't have to be explicit. That doesn't matter to me. So again, it's back to that "detail." I'm looking for a nuance, and I'm totally satisfied with a nuance.

Based on some of her examples, we had assumed that "lift" would include things the person says, but Kendall corrects us. She is attending to—and satisfied with—nuances of expressions and tonality.

Kendall's Evidence, then, is "I feel filled up inside (in my upper body), the energy feels very 'forward,' I'm eager to tell them something, and they 'brighten'; there is some verbal or non-verbal 'lift'."

6

Beliefs: Cause-Effects

While the equivalence relationships we create identify what things *are* (this *means* that), the causal relationships we create specify how things *affect* each other: this *causes* that. If you think of equivalence relationships as the threads of your experience, then causal relationships are the weaving of those threads. Together they create the fabric of your reality. If we want to reproduce a particular tapestry, it is essential to have both the correct threads *and* to know how to correctly weave those threads together.

If we were reproducing an actual fabric it would be tedious to individually specify each and every intertwining of threads as we recreate the whole piece. It is more efficient to identify the *patterns* of how the threads are woven. Similarly, we do not want to identify every twist and turn in our exemplar's thinking and experience. Rather, we want to discover those patterns of cause-effects that govern how those twists and turns are taken.

Enabling Cause-Effect

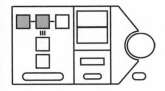

"Dreaming won't get you to Damascus, sir, but discipline will."

Maj. Allenby advising Prince Feisal
in *Lawrence of Arabia*

Because a Criterion is an important standard that you want satisfied you will naturally learn from your life experiences what enables it to *be* satisfied. For instance, if it is important to you to "Be Understood," your life experiences may have taught you that *I need to express myself simply and directly* **in order to** *be understood*. The need to satisfy a Criterion motivates us to learn the cause-effects regarding what must be true, what we must do, or what must happen in order for that Criterion to be satisfied. Some examples:

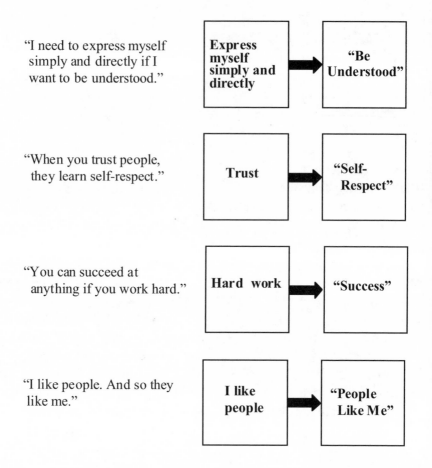

"I need to express myself simply and directly if I want to be understood."

"When you trust people, they learn self-respect."

"You can succeed at anything if you work hard."

"I like people. And so they like me."

If we consider Criteria as destinations, then these cause-effects map the routes. They are our beliefs about the way to get us to the destination: if you want to get to "self-respect," you get there via *trust,* the road to "success" is paved with hard *work,* and so on.

Whatever the cause-effect may be, its impact is to organize our behavior along certain lines. The person who believes "When you trust people, they learn self-respect" will naturally endeavor to trust others; the person who believes "You can succeed at anything if you work hard" will naturally endeavor to work hard. These *enabling* cause-effects reveal the kinds of things a person is likely to try to do in order to satisfy her Criterion:

> The Enabling Cause-Effect *specifies the conditions believed necessary to satisfy the Criterion.*

"Conditions" covers a lot of ground. The range of what can serve as an Enabling Cause-Effect is as broad as experience itself. It can be anything from the grandest abstraction ("It is living a philosophy of 'oneness' that makes transcendence possible"), to the humblest particular ("Telling someone that they are likeable makes them feel good"). Despite the enormous difference in specificity between "philosophy of 'oneness'" and "telling someone they are likeable," both statements reveal what these people try to make happen, look for, or do in order to satisfy their Criterion.

Of course, two people can have the same Criterion but different Enabling Causes. What you believe to be the Enabling Cause-Effect relationship for a particular Criterion will depend upon your personal history. For instance, when it comes to being understood, instead of "be simple and direct," your life experience may have taught you that *I need to see my own ideas clearly* in order to be understood." Or perhaps "*I must wait until people are in a sufficiently receptive mood* in order to be understood." Or perhaps "*I need to believe in what I am saying* in order to be understood." Remember that the Enabling Cause-Effect expresses what *this* particular person (exemplar) believes is a prerequisite to having her Criterion satisfied.

Elicitation Questions for the Enabling Cause-Effect

"What enables someone to [Criterion]?"
— or —
"What is necessary for there to be [Criterion]?"

EXAMPLES

Q: What enables someone to "include everyone"?

Adam: You have to **know the group**. Without that, you can't really know what they will naturally enjoy and respond to.

Q: What is necessary for there to be "movement"?

Bridgit: **Trust.** If you **trust the child to know how much she can handle at any one time**, you will be able to help her move. And whenever there is movement, I always praise her.

Q: What is necessary for there to be "elegance" in a web site?

Claire: If we are talking elegance, it has to be easy and smooth to

> navigate. And if you're going to get that, you have to *care
> more about the experience of the end user than about
> being clever, getting lost in your own cleverness*.

When eliciting the Enabling Cause-Effect it is important to keep in mind that we are capturing a *belief* about how the world works; it is the exemplar's generalization about what conditions help make it possible for her Criterion to be satisfied. We need to remember this distinction because it may happen that the exemplar does not give us her generalization about what is necessary, but instead starts describing the various things she *actually does* when manifesting her Ability. That is, she starts describing her Strategy (which we will explore in detail in Chapter 8.)

For example, Adam's belief, "You have to know the group," tells us what condition he believes must be satisfied in order to ensure that people are included; it does not tell us the various actions he takes in order to operationalize that belief, such as sending out a questionnaire, meeting each person privately for a talk, getting a supervisor's assessment of them, and gathering information about their cultural and social backgrounds (all of which may be parts of his Strategy).

One way to determine whether your exemplar is describing her Enabling Cause-Effect or elements of her Strategy is to ask yourself, Does her answer tell me what specifically to do (if so, it is probably Strategy) or is it more of a goal or intention that could be pursued in many different ways (in which case it is probably Enabling Cause-Effect)?

"Being Passionate About Something" – Eliciting the Enabling Cause-Effect

Since it is important to Kendall to "Be Appreciative," she probably has beliefs about what leads to that being possible:

> David: What makes it possible for someone to be appreciative?
> What makes it possible for someone to notice the
> detailed things that other people do that are special? In
> general, you know, what *makes* that possible—
>
> Kendall: *You have to pay attention.*
>
> David: You have to pay attention.
>
> Kendall: Yeah, they have to pay attention. I mean, *if you're
> looking for details and nuances, you have to pay*

> ***attention to what's happening right there***. And I think
> it's really easy—it's actually easier for people to get lost
> in their own internal dialogue, and then they miss things.
> So they have to either quiet that dialogue or shift the
> dialogue so that it's instead—whatever they're doing—
> asking themselves a question that helps them pay
> attention.

David: Okay, great.

Kendall: Like, you can't *miss* it, it's so fleeting, these details. You
can't miss them.

David: You grab 'em.

Kendall: But they're always there. Yeah. It's like, There's one,
there's one! I don't know if it's grabbing. It's more
pointing out. But yeah.

As you can see and hear in the DVD presentation, Kendall's answer, "You
have to pay attention," almost erupts from her. The quality of her voice
tonality and her gestures announce *This is it*. Coming as it does on the heels
of being unsure about what she is being asked, this is a good example of the
kind of behavior (tonality and gestures) that lets you know that what your
exemplar is saying is *true* for her.

Her Enabling Cause-Effect is interesting in that it reveals that being
appreciative is something she is *working* to do. Many people are appreciative
when the world gives them something to appreciate; it is a passive response to
something which has met their criteria. For Kendall, however, being
appreciative is an active pursuit ("you pay attention") of what is already there
("the details are always there").

When she talks about shifting internal dialogue by asking questions she is
describing an internal behavior that she uses to help her pay attention; that is,
it is one of the ways she puts her Enabling Cause-Effect into action. So this is
a bit of her Strategy, and not part of the Enabling Cause-Effect itself.

Motivating Cause-Effect

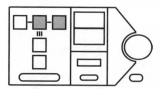

The most important motive for work in school and in life is pleasure in work, pleasure in its result, and the knowledge of the value of the result to the community.

– Albert Einstein

Being capable of doing something is not the same thing as being willing to do it. Both capability and willingness are necessary for an ability to manifest itself.

All of us have examples of knowing what we want or need to do, but still not do it. Consequently, we often think of ourselves as being weak or slothful, fearful of the unpleasantness of hard work, of risks, or even of simple unfamiliarity. Rusting exercise equipment, dusty piano keys, stacks of unread books, overgrown gardens, snow drifts of unpaid bills, fading voices of friends, swallowed insults, poor negotiations, missed investments, unwritten books…all mutely shake their fingers at us in reproach.

The fact is that none of us has enough time and energy to make everything equally important. We necessarily pursue fulfilling some goals, and leave others for "later." This does not mean we pursue only what is easy. We *do* tackle many things that are difficult, unpleasant, or unfamiliar, sometimes taking on even onerous tasks with eagerness and determination. How does that happen?

Recently, a colleague of ours felt he had to say no to a project that he had previously agreed to do. He knew he would greatly disappoint the other people involved, and knew it would be unpleasant to do so. What motivated him to tell the hard truth? "It was a matter of self-respect. I didn't feel I could respect myself if I didn't tell them the truth." For him, "self-respect" was intrinsically important and more compelling than his fear of disappointing his colleagues.

Think of something you did recently even though it was difficult or unpleasant. Now consider, Why did you do it? Like our colleague, you had a reason that was compelling enough to motivate you to do it. Typically, that reason was connected to something intrinsically important to *you*. In fact, it is likely that it expressed or related to some aspect of who you are, so it was naturally compelling. We call these compelling personal values (ideals, standards, principles) *Prime Motivators*. The causal relationship between a Prime Motivator and a Criterion is the *Motivating Cause-Effect*:

The Motivating Cause-Effect *is the connection*

between satisfying the Criterion and satisfying a
Prime Motivator.

In a Motivating Cause-Effect, satisfying the Criterion contributes or leads to fulfilling something larger, something intrinsically important to you; typically, this will be one of your Prime Motivators. Or, to describe this cause-effect relationship the other way around, the need or desire to fulfill a Prime Motivator motivates you to pursue satisfying the Criterion. For our colleague the Motivating Cause-Effect relationship is, "It is necessary to be honest with myself and with others in order to respect myself":

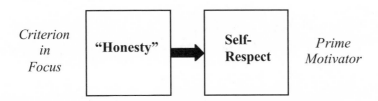

In fact, both sides of the Motivating Cause-Effect are criteria (that is, both are important standards of evaluation). They serve different functions, however. The Criterion in focus establishes what is essential to evaluate and satisfy when operating in a specific context (in our example, "honesty," when speaking with colleagues). A Prime Motivator, on the other hand, is something that is essential to fulfill *across most or all contexts*. For our colleague, "self-respect" is essential not only when he is interacting with his colleagues, but also when considering the meaning of life, vying for parking spaces, and on and on.

Because Prime Motivators are often descriptive of personal identity, and are often subjectively experienced as "deeper," "higher," "what it's all about," or "more me" than are context-specific Criteria. (Indeed, Prime Motivators are often criteria that go to the very core of who we are: self-concept, identity, personality, soul.)

Elicitation Questions for the Motivating Cause-Effect

"Why is [Criterion] important?"

— or —

"What does [Criterion] lead to or make possible?"

EXAMPLES

Q: Why is it important that "everyone is included"?

Adam: If they are included they will sort of all feed their excitement and joy into each other, and the celebration becomes an opportunity to **become a real community**.

Q: What does "movement" lead to or make possible?

Bridgit: **Freedom**, actually. As long as you're moving, you have **the possibility of going anywhere**.

Q: Why is "elegance" important?

Claire: If you can flow through a site then that site **makes sense**. It drives me nuts when things don't **make sense**.

In some cases you will find that an exemplar's Criterion and Motivator are one and the same. That is, the Criterion in focus when she is manifesting her Ability is also a Prime Motivator. In these instances the Criterion is itself as important as things get for this person; it is not in service of anything higher or deeper. If this were true for Adam when planning a celebration, for example, "Inclusion" would be both his Criterion *and* his Prime Motivator.

It is likely that your exemplar's Criterion and Prime Motivator are one and the same when, no matter how many times you persist in asking the elicitation question "Why is the [Criterion] important?" your exemplar...

* Answers each time with different re-phrasings of that same Criterion.

* Is stumped and cannot come up with anything that the Criterion is in service of.

* Says things like, "Well, it just is," "What else is there?" or "That's just what life's about."

"Being Passionate About Something" – Eliciting the Motivating Cause-Effect

David: Why is it important to be appreciative? Why is it important to notice these detailed things that people do that are special?

Kendall: I've always said, because my whole life is about ***loving
and being loved***. So that's why it's important to me. It's
just to love and be loved...Why else is it important...It's
fun. (laughs) It beats focusing on all the, you know, crap
that's out there in the world.

In her response, Kendall explains that "loving and being loved" is what
"my whole life is about." As we noted above, phrases like this mark out Prime
Motivators. So we know that "loving and being loved" is at least part of her
Motivating Cause-Effect.

She then continues to search ("Why else is it important...?"), and comes
up with "fun." Her analogue—tonality, gestures, expressions—reveal that fun
is something that is important to her, but it is not the primary issue when it
comes to being passionate. She would be willing to forego fun if that were
necessary to support loving and being loved, but she is not going to forego
loving and being loved so she can have fun.

Also, notice that her Prime Motivator presupposes something that is
ongoing and endless: "lov*ing* and be*ing* loved." This is subjectively quite
different than if it were, "To love and be loved," which suggests a goal to be
attained. Once goals are attained, they tend to lose their power to motivate us.
Kendall's ongoing and endless Prime Motivator, however, supports the
ability to be passionate about something, which is typically a long term—
often life-long—devotion.

7

Supporting Beliefs

Like all of us, the exemplar is operating within an endless web of beliefs. Because it *is* an endless web, we want to focus on only those beliefs that are necessary to be able to manifest the exemplar's Ability. Most of the necessary beliefs will be variations on a few underlying themes, which we capture in the Belief Template.

However, this does not mean that beliefs not already captured in the Belief Template are inconsequential. They are certainly of some consequence to the exemplar. They contribute in many subtle ways to her perceptions, choices, experience, and behavior when manifesting her Ability. While these beliefs may not be essential to the structure that makes that Ability possible, some of them may still be *helpful* to us in taking it on. We call these, *Supporting Beliefs*:

> Supporting Beliefs *are beliefs that significantly*
> *support the person in manifesting the Array.*

Unlike the Criterion and its Belief Template, we do not go hunting for Supporting Beliefs. If you go hunting for beliefs, you will always find them. Lots of them. Instead we *notice* when Supporting Beliefs are there. Once in awhile a particular belief jumps out of the crowd of background equivalences and cause-effects. Because we are *not* looking for every member in the crowd of beliefs, when one suddenly stands out there is good reason to take notice of it and to consider how significant it is to the exemplar's Ability. Beliefs that tend to stand out are often those that come neatly packaged in a clear and assertive statement, much like an epigram ("Look before you leap" "He who hesitates is lost").

For example, a colleague was modeling an exemplar's ability to generate ideas for remodeling a home. She had already identified the exemplar's Belief Template, when he declared:

> "If it's been made, it can be changed."

Our colleague recognized immediately that this was not only a belief that significantly supported her exemplar's ability to come up with remodeling ideas, but that it was a belief that she herself had not previously held. When she then imagined remodeling while holding that belief, she discovered that her own ability to use the exemplar's Belief Template and strategies immediately and dramatically improved. Consequently, she added "If it's been made, it can be changed" to the model as a Supporting Belief.

In some cases there may be several Supporting Beliefs that significantly enhance the manifesting of an Ability. In one of our modeling seminars, for instance, Dee was modeling "Authentic and Respectful Straight-Talking." The Criterion and its Belief Template were:

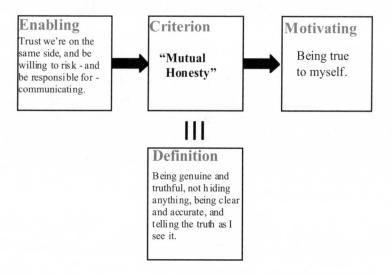

Some of the Supporting Beliefs she identified were:

"Conversation is catalytic in nature."
"Honesty has more value than comfort."
"We are all human and are all doing our best."
"People deserve to be able to talk about things. It's a gift to them."

None of these are found in the Belief Template for "Authentic and respectful straight-talking," and none of them is necessary in order to operate out of that Belief Template. But when you imagine operating out of it while also holding any or all of these Supporting Beliefs you will discover that they significantly intensify your experience and increase your ease in manifesting the Ability. Taking on your exemplar's Supporting Beliefs will give you greater depth and make the Ability more robust from the outset.

Noticing Supporting Beliefs

As we said, Supporting Beliefs are not elicited, but noticed. Because they appear fortuitously, elicitation involves noticing that you have been *grabbed* by a statement from your exemplar. Usually you are grabbed because the belief is expressed in a punchy, evocative, or epigrammatic form. If when you try on that belief it also significantly facilitates manifesting the Ability, it is worth noting as a Supporting Belief.

EXAMPLES

Adam: *No one wants to be left out—they just want to be asked in the right way.*

Bridgit: *Think like a child and you will know what to do.*

Claire: *When it comes to the Internet, what annoys you probably annoys everyone else, too.*

"Being Passionate About Something" – *Noticing the Supporting Beliefs*

Many times during the elicitation, Kendall talked about "searching." (For example, "I'm searching, or scanning very often, with riding, or with my husband, or with clients...") So when, toward the end of the elicitation, she came out with an emphatic statement about searching, it struck us as possibly significant. She was talking about her search to find something to be passionate about:

Kendall: So, keeping my eye out. And at times it was really frustrating not to have that.

David: You wanted it *now*.

Kendall: I just wanted it. Yeah, I did want it now. I wanted it already! [laughs] So I just had to console myself and say, It'll be there. *It's* **there**. *I just need to keep searching.*

When we tried on the belief "It's *there*. I just need to keep searching," it significantly increased our ability to be appreciative, notice what is special. and pay attention (all elements of her Belief Template). And so we include it in the Array as a Supporting Belief.

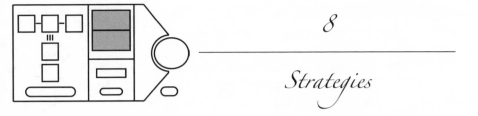

8

Strategies

We do a lot of things. We get out of bed on time, sort priorities, organize our day's work, find necessary information, correctly spell a word, deliver bad news to the boss, engage an audience, get the kids to clean their rooms, exercise, make financial decisions, select birthday gifts, plan meals, choose wisely from the menu, and come up with solutions to vexing problems. These are all things we do, and we do them through various combinations of thinking and behavior.

This thinking and behaving is not random. The thinking and behaving we do to get out of bed on time is specific for that purpose; it involves considerations and behaviors that are different than those we engage in when selecting a birthday gift for a friend or dealing with the boss. Whatever the desired outcome may be, we gather information, sort perceptions, generate ideas, pose questions, make statements, push buttons, twist images, chew words, and check our feelings...all in service of attaining that outcome. That is, we employ a *strategy*. You may well be unaware of all of the internal and external actions that make up one of your strategies. Nevertheless, they are there, generating the impact you have on your world:

> Strategies *are sets and sequences of internal processes and external behaviors intended to attain particular outcomes.*

All of us have numerous strategies for dealing with the countless small and large outcomes, goals, and needs that flow through our daily lives. However, just because we have a strategy for something does not mean it is a good strategy. Some strategies work better than others. One of the primary reasons that some people are especially good at a particular ability is that they are using effective strategies.

It is essential to recognize the importance of internal processes in having strategies that are effective. Obviously there is a difference between moving furniture in a room and moving furniture in your head; moving furniture in your head does not, in and of itself affect anything in the world outside of you. Like moving furniture in the room, however, doing it in your head *does* involve taking action, though this is in the form of *internal processes*. These internal processes include computation, representation, spatial manipulation, internal dialogue, internal questions, sensations, memory sorting, shifts in perspective, and so on. It is for this reason that trying to model an exemplar solely by emulating her external behavior rarely works; the exemplar is doing things that go beyond what we observe in her behavior. She is also *doing* on the inside, and those internal processes are also informing and guiding her external behavior.

The relative importance of external behaviors and internal processes depends upon the ability being modeled. Multiplying numbers in one's head will certainly involve the operation of a lot of internal processes and few external behaviors. On the other hand, the ability to sink baskets with a basketball requires the operation of many more external behaviors.

Furthermore, the mix of external behaviors and internal processes may vary between exemplars. In modeling the ability of architects to come up with ideas for home design, for example, we might discover that one architect imagines various combinations of shapes, volumes, and lines until she finds a basic set that fits her client's desires and personality. Another architect wanders around the actual home site, imagining possible shapes and walking "in" them until he finds those that fit his client's desires and personality. The first architect's strategy involves primarily internal processes, and the strategy of the second architect involves a mix of both internal processes and external behaviors.

Sequences and Sets

Strategies are usually thought of as a sequence of steps: do this, then do this, then this, then this, and so on. And many strategies are just like that; sequences of operations that take the form of recipes, algorithms, formulas, steps, procedures, and techniques for achieving desired outcomes. Cooking recipes, determining the income tax you owe the government, and planting a garden are familiar examples of such strategies. (Sugar must be creamed into the butter *before* adding the eggs; the tax percentage is applied to your income *after* subtracting your deductions; soil is turned over and soil amendments added *before* seeding.)

The sequential strategy of the architect in the above example may run something like this: interview the homeowners to discover what experiences they want to have in their home, *then* go to the site at different times of the day and night, *then* walk around it until you know it from every angle, *then* begin to imagine shapes and forms that fit with the desires of the clients, *then* actually walk "inside" those shapes to determine if they are likely to fit with the client, *then*... Like beads on a string, each step in such strategies is a prerequisite for effectively taking the step that follows.

But not all strategies can be beaded onto the string of sequence. Many strategies instead involve a *set* of internal processes and external behaviors. In these strategies there is not a first, second, and third step to take, but a group of steps that are taken either simultaneously or in an ad hoc fashion. For instance, a strategy for safe driving might involve: look several hundred feet ahead and imagine how driving conditions might be changing for you; maintain sufficient stopping distance between you and the car in front; leave yourself a space to go either to the left or to the right in case of an emergency; check mirrors every few seconds; shift your body enough to keep it loose and relaxed... This is not a sequential strategy, but a set of behaviors which are enacted as needed, sometimes sequentially and at other times simultaneously.

Primary Strategy

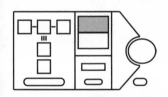

"Don't you see, Bloom, darling Bloom, glorious Bloom? It's so simple. Step one: you find the worst play in the world, a surefire flop. Step two: I raise a million bucks. (There are a lot of little old ladies in the world.) Step three: you go back to work on the books, only list the backers one for the government and one for us. You can do it, Bloom. You're a wizard. Step four: we open on Broadway, and, before you can say step five, we close on Broadway. Step six: we take our million bucks and we fly to Rio de Janeiro! Rio, Rio-by-the-sea-o..."

Zero Mostel hatching his fool-proof
plan in Mel Brooks' *The Producers*

One of the qualities that makes a person an exemplar of a particular Ability is that she uses a strategy that consistently works. In the course of her life experiences she has acquired the internal processes and external behaviors that make it possible to be effective in a certain context. We call those internal and external actions that bring an Ability to life the *Primary Strategy*:

> The Primary Strategy is *the set of internal processes*
> *and external behaviors that are usually effective in*
> *manifesting the Ability.*

What makes a Strategy *primary* is that it consists of those intern?

external actions with which the exemplar always leads. Your exemplar leads with those particular internal and external actions for the very good reason that those particular internal processes and external behaviors *work*.

Elicitation Questions for the Primary Strategy

> **"What are you usually doing—on the 'inside' and on the 'outside'—to [Ability]?"**
> — or —
> **"How do you normally go about [Ability]?"**

EXAMPLES

Q: What are you usually doing—on the "inside" and on the "outside"— to plan a celebration?

Adam: *If I don't already know the people who will be coming—I mean their sub-culture, age range, where from, social and work background, their relationships with each other, and so on—I find out. I also find out what the agenda is for the celebration. Then, for each of the events on the agenda, I imagine I'm one of the people attending—not as me, but as them—and ask myself, "What do I wish would be happening here now?" And then I imagine whoever is coming who is likely not to feel comfortable and part of the group, and ask myself, "What would draw me into this?" I take those two answers and figure out how to make sure both happen...*

Q: What are you usually doing—on the "inside" and on the "outside"— to be patient with a child?

Bridgit: Several things. *I'm always noticing what the child can do already. I consider what would be a small step from there toward where she eventually needs to be in her learning. And we take just that step. If she's pleased with that, it goes smoothly, we can take the next step. I'm always ¬aying close attention to her attention level and comfort. ¬long as these are okay, we can keep going. And when ¬oves forward in any way, I make sure to let her know* *tha*t, so she can be proud of herself, which, of course, she has every right to be...

Q: How do you normally go about designing the user interface for a web site?

Claire: *I just blank myself out, set Claire aside for awhile. I come to this web site like it's my very first visit, and as someone who is naïve about the web. And I notice, where do my eyes go? Do I have to search for what I want?, which is a problem. Is there stuff I would never use, or at least not here? Also a problem. I also ask myself, how can this whatever-it-is be misunderstood? If it's a search problem, I move things around until it is right where my naïve self can find it easily. If it's something superfluous, I put it either on another page or (if at all possible) in the trash can. And stuff that can be misunderstood...well, if it's a graphic, I work with the graphics people to clean it up, and if it's text, the writers...*

Adam's Primary Strategy for planning a celebration is essentially sequential:

1. Find out who is coming and the agenda of events.
2. For each event, imagine I am an attendee and ask myself, "What do I wish would be happening here now?"
3. Imagine I am an uncomfortable attendee and ask myself, "What would draw me into this?"
4. Take those two answers and figure out how to make sure both happen.
5. [Etc.]

Bridgit and Claire's Primary Strategies are more simultaneous, involving steps that are taken as the situation calls for them. Claire's Primary Strategy, for instance, is made up of the following *ad hoc* elements:

* If it's a search problem, I move things around until it is right where my naïve self can find it easily.
* If it's something superfluous, I put it either on another page or (if at all possible) in the trash can.

      *   Stuff that can be misunderstood…well, if it's a graphic, I work with the graphics people to clean it up, and if it's text, the writers.

One thing that becomes apparent as we elicit a Primary Strategy—or any strategy—is that there are endless layers of details that we could delve into. Since we cannot mine every one of these layers, how specific do we need to be when getting a description of a strategy?

There is no set level of specificity that is the right level. A Strategy step that is too big does not give us the detail we need in order to know what to do; a Strategy step that is too small burdens us with unnecessary detail. The right level of specificity is that which allows you to manifest the Strategy yourself.

When you elicit the Primary Strategy, your goal is to specify it to a level of detail that fits with your *current level of competence*. You do this by asking yourself, "Can I do this step from the exemplar's description of it?" For instance, if a step in the exemplar's Primary Strategy is to "imagine the future I want," and you already know how to do that, there is probably no need to go any further into its details. If instead you do not know how to "imagine the future I want," then you *do* need to go deeper into its details. That is, you need to ask your exemplar for more details until you arrive at a level of internal processes and external behaviors at which you are (or can easily become) competent.[1]

"Being Passionate About Something" – Eliciting the Primary Strategy

Most Primary Strategies are relatively simple and straightforward, like those of Adam, Bridgit, and Claire. Kendall's Primary Strategy, however, turned out to be a bit more complicated, as we discovered the first time we asked her about what she does to be passionate about her work:

    David: We can use as a starting place your work again, that you are passionate about your coaching—

    Kendall: It's not really coaching, it's really helping people.

    David: So helping people.

    Kendall: It's helping people.

    David: You're passionate about helping people.

---

[1] Of course, you may still want to explore and consider how your exemplar takes a strategy step with which you are already competent. After all, your exemplar may do it differently, and if so, knowing what she does may extend and enrich your own competency.

Kendall: Yep. Absolutely.

David: Good. Thank you. Alright. What are you normally doing on the inside and on the outside in order to help people?

Kendall: *I'm listening. I mean really, really listening intently to what they're saying—in other words, the sound of their words—and what they're saying. And I'm listening for…it's like I'm doing a check: Is there any deeper meaning here? Is there a pattern here?*

David: Okay.

Kendall: Yeah. And sometimes the answer is, No. What they said is just what they said and, fine, we move on. It's not like I'm trying to artificially find meaning in every single thing someone says. *I'm just checking to see, do I think there's more meaning here? And if there is, I usually, just about 100% of the time, I stop and check it out with them.*

David: If there is or you think there is.

Kendall: Right. *And the other thing I'm doing, with my work, is… I'm constantly—I shouldn't say constantly—I'm periodically double checking that I'm paying attention.* You know, I mean, I'm as prone to having my mind wander as anybody else. I just think I catch it faster than a lot of people do. And I notice a lot with—*I use my body posture a lot to help with that. So I do tend to sit up straight, or I lean a little forward. I'm relaxed and I'm breathing, but I'm not slouched back. I tend to see them in front of me, even though they're physically not* because, really, 100% of my work is on the telephone. And people have said, How can you do that, when all you have is a voice? I say, well, it's easy. Because *I picture them right there with me [gesturing], right in front of me.* So that's actually part of the strategy, too, in paying this really—I mean I have to say I think I pay exquisite attention to people. Or I'm *not*. [laughs] Or I'm not paying attention at all. Not to a client, but with my family or with my husband, you know, because I'm paying exquisite attention to something else. So it's being very focused and there's definitely…*I become aware that*

> *there's definitely something about keeping my visual field like this [demonstrating], fairly narrow. Unless I need to be creative. Then I make sure and widen it.*

David: Great.

Kendall: And the reason I *know* this is because I've had times where I've had difficulty, either I'm distracted because I've got other projects, or I'm tired, or I've been working with too many people, whatever, so I've had to work harder to pay that kind of attention that I expect of myself. And so I've had to figure out how to do that. So that I can do it when it's not quite as, um, unconscious.

> *Somewhere in there, too, is, you know, this thing of noticing the details. I notice what I'm enjoying.* I notice the details of what I'm enjoying. So for example, with work I'll think—I'll say to myself, This is so cool! I get to stay home with my headset and people pay me to help them out!

We could have approached Kendall's Primary Strategy as one, big strategy. It seemed to us, however, that it would be clearer and more useful to divide it into three "sub" strategies: "Pay attention," "Look for deeper meaning," and "Enjoy the details." So we took them one at a time, treating each element as a Strategy in its own right:

"PAY ATTENTION"

David: So, what are you doing on the inside or the outside to keep yourself attentive when you're…actually, with your horses, with your husband, or at work?

Kendall: *I'm sitting forward*…which actually with riding isn't exactly how I want to sit, so that's always been a struggle for me. But *it's sitting forward—so I'm not leaning back—and there's probably a certain amount of tension in my body of readiness*. And, when I'm paying attention—it happens so often and so fast, it's a little hard to distinguish, but there's…it's like *I'm seeing the big picture and at the same time seeing the details*. So if I'm working with somebody, *I'm seeing the big picture of where we're going*. You know, they're paying me to make progress. And so *I'm checking in, Are we still making progress towards the…in the direction we want to go in?* Which is, for my clients, getting more clients. They want to have more clients.

David: So "big picture" includes, "Where is it we want to be going?"

Kendall: Right. *I'm constantly checking in, Are we making progress towards that big picture?* I'm not particular, necessarily, about the progress being—about measuring the progress. *I don't measure the progress; I just want there to be progress.* There has to have a sense of action happening. *And then I'm checking in with the details to, you know, sorting for, okay, if what we're talking about right now, is it moving us toward this big picture? So this is a little different than finding meaning. This is just about paying attention.*

David: Right.

Kendall goes into a bit more detail regarding the role her posture plays in paying attention. But what really comes out this time is the central importance of holding "the big picture." By attending to the details of what is going on in her experience, she can measure—in an *ongoing* way— "progress" in relation to "the big picture."

Now we need to find out two things. First, is "holding the big picture" relevant only in the context of working with her clients, or is it something Kendall does whenever she is being passionate about something? Second, if this *is* a pattern, what is "holding the big picture" in *general* (that is, in situations other than with her clients)? We answer both of these questions by having her compare her experience across all three examples of being passionate:

David: Is it the case then, that with Jaggy, you also, you have a big picture in relation to him—

Kendall: Yes. Right.

David: In terms of—I don't know, I'm not a horse rider—

Kendall: *Let's say I'm doing my dressage training, and so I have…I know that over all—so it's "big picture," "over all," same thing—that we need to work on more flexibility to the right.* That's what we need to work on. So then I start, you know, I create the details about the different movements and the exercises I can do, and the different things that I need to pay attention to in my body. So I'm constantly checking in there. *And when you're dealing with an animal—just like with a human being—I think you have to be flexible.* Because I may want to work on a particular thing with my horse and he's not—that's not what's going to work for him that day. You know, I expect this much of a range [hands wide] and his range that day is this much [hands close]. And that's—so I have to adjust. And the same thing happens with a client.

She confirms that she holds a big picture in relation to her riding. (Kendall also makes a point about the need for flexibility as she pays attention. This makes sense in that paying attention means being responsive to what is there, rather than trying to cause something to be there.) We still want to check whether or not "holding the big picture" is also part of her strategy for being passionate about her relationship with her husband:

David: Is it the case with your husband that you have a big picture of, say, what you would like your relationship to *be* with him, or what you would like for him to have for himself? Is there a big picture in relation to him?

Kendall: *Yes. It's not as well defined as these others, but it's a picture of, of staying very loving with each other—is first and foremost—and the big picture of really appreciating him [laughs], really appreciating him, and me being appreciated, too, actually. So it's much more generalized.*

David: I see. Okay.

Kendall: I don't have goals with our relationship. I mean, it's not like that. No. So actually it's more at a detailed level. If there's any little glitch, we talk and work it through.

David: Yeah. It's more like you're *in* the big picture.

Kendall: Right, right.

David: And it's *keeping* yourself in that big picture—

Kendall: Correct.

David: —through attention to those details.

Kendall: Yes. That's a good way to put it.

So, in each of the contexts in which she is passionate she is holding a big picture, and her big picture is of what she generally wants to have happen or be true in each of those contexts.

Kendall goes on to describe the strategic role of asking herself questions when paying attention:

Kendall: You know what it is, I go back to asking—because in my mind I'm always—*part of paying attention for me is always asking questions. I think a lot in questions. And so, yeah, I go back to asking questions either in my mind or verbally. It doesn't matter which it is.*

David: And, so, are there certain questions, or certain kinds of questions you ask, or is it in order to get yourself back to being attentive—

Kendall: No, it's—

David: The *effect* of asking questions—

Kendall: Right.

David: —is to bring your attention back to the present.

Kendall: Right. *Because when I've fallen out of paying attention, I'm usually not asking myself questions; I'm usually telling myself about other stuff.* Usually I'm worrying about something.

David: Great.

Kendall: Yeah, it's very different than asking questions. And so actually my riding, I ask a lot of questions also. I ask questions constantly, which is how I improved so much, [laughs] you know.

David: So is that part of *keeping* attentive, is that—

Kendall: Asking questions.

David: Asking questions.

Kendall: And it doesn't have to be…some of them I ask out loud.

You know, percentage wise, I'm probably asking a third of the questions that I'm thinking of.

David: Mm hm.

Kendall: So, to translate that to riding, when I'm riding I'm asking questions of my own body posture. Are my elbows at my sides? you know, whatever…It depends on what I'm working on. Right now I'm working on not letting the reins slip through my hands, because I have a bad habit of doing that. So I'm just asking the question, Do I have my thumb enough on the reins? Are my arms still loose? So I just ask that question over and over and over again. And it's like, Oop! That allows me to make little corrections. Then I also ask questions about my horse. Is he falling on his shoulder? Is he straight? Is he, you know, does he feel relaxed in his body? *So I'm asking all these different questions. And it's just like [snapping her fingers] constant.*

"LOOK FOR DEEPER MEANING"

We opened our inquiry into how Kendall finds deeper meaning by reminding her that, in describing her client work, she had mentioned "listening to something in the person's voice that indicates that there is a deeper meaning":

Kendall: I'm usually listening for—it's actually their words rather than the voice. *A lot of times I'm listening for something that they've noticed or something that they've done.* So, for example, this is a kind of a bigger picture example, but a client will come to the call and they'll start in by saying, "Okay, today I want to work on blah, blah, blah, blah, blah and, by the way, I got a couple of new clients last week, but what I really want to work on is this over here." And I'll say, "Okay, wait a second. Did I just hear you say you got two new clients last week?" And they'll say, "Yes." And I'll tell them, "Let's just stop for a moment," and "I have questions about that." And, in a way, what I'm thinking is—from a practical basis I want to find out how those people find them and all that—but also, *let's celebrate this. This is important. Don't just skip it.*

David: So you listen for something that they've noticed or done that's in some way different or new or—

Kendall: Right, *even if it's tiny...tiny, tiny. That's the nuance there. Any little bit of a forward movement or a stretch, or a discovery or an Aha.* And so often people just sail right through it. I want to know, you know, *How is this important to you? What does this mean for you?* So, if they bring something to the conversation that they already know is meaningful *I tend to ask something, ask a question so that it deepens the meaning even more...I really think I'm, I'm searching, or scanning very often, with riding, or with my husband, or with clients, searching for...back to that thing: I'm searching for what is meaningful, I'm searching for clues.*

David: So, you want to know—when you recognize, this person has revealed to you in some way, that they've made some bit of forward movement or some stretch of some kind—you want to know, how is this important to the person? If there *is* forward movement or there *is* a stretch, it must *be* important.

Kendall: Right. *It actually could be backwards movement, and that's important, too.*

David: Right. Movement's important.

Kendall: *Movement is really important.* I'm very proactive.

When it comes to finding "the deeper meaning," Kendall is looking for anything that indicates "movement" of some kind. Even the tiniest bit of movement—a detail or nuance—is potentially indicative of something meaningful.

When she notices something possibly meaningful, she asks questions such as, "How is this important to you? What does this mean for you?" Later in the elicitation we confirmed that she asks these same questions when she's being passionate about riding or about her relationship with her husband.

"ENJOY THE DETAILS"

As we discovered in her strategy for finding the deeper meaning, Kendall is very attentive to details. Details are not simply information, however, but something she enjoys and even celebrates, as well:

Kendall: I love the way my saddle feels, and so I'll get into the saddle and, instead of just moving on, I think—and sometimes I'll say it out loud—"This saddle feels *great*." And it somehow connects me to the deeper meaning of how much I really enjoy riding.

David: You're noticing—

Kendall: *I'm noticing.* With the feel of the air when it's crisp— I love riding when it's crisp, and the way it feels on my face. I don't get the sense of hair streaming because I braid my hair up so it doesn't get tangled. And I wear a helmet. But, yeah, the feel of the leather. The smells. There's a lot, particularly with horses there's a lot with smell.

David: You know what you enjoy.

Kendall: *I know what I enjoy.*

David: Then you notice it.

Kendall: *I'm looking for evidence to reinforce what I enjoy.* So even when I used to do a lot of horse shows, which I don't anymore, but when I did them they were very exhausting. And I would be dead tired on my feet and dirty and grimy and sweaty from a very long day at the horse show. And I'd think...I would just notice, and relish, the sensation of being dirty and grimy and sweaty having spent time all day at this horse show. So even those types of things which are not necessarily pleasant, *I somehow turn them into feeding my enjoyment. And that has to happen, otherwise I lose interest. If it's unpleasant, especially if it's repetitively unpleasant, I'm not going to do it.*

David: It's as though I have made a *decision* to enjoy my life.

Kendall: Yes.

David: It's not about, Well, I'd *like* to, or I *should*—

Kendall: No, no.

David: I've decided, I'm going to enjoy my life.

Kendall: Correct.

David: And *this* is what I enjoy. These are the things I know give me enjoyment.

Kendall: Right. And if I'm missing something—because I try and have everything in my life meet this type of criteria, so *if I am finding myself not enjoying my life then I decide to do something about it. I don't just live with it. And it goes down to even a small chunk level. If I'm riding and I'm too tired to really school my horse, then I will decide to just enjoy just walking on him, and noticing the birds and the trees and the sounds* and...

David: There's always some small bit or piece that you *could* put your attention on and appreciate.

Kendall: Oh absolutely. Yes.

[...]

David: You're storing, Oh, these are things there are to appreciate in Debbie!

Kendall: Right. I think that's actually very true. I'm just trying that on because...it's like *I'm cataloguing that, and storing it somewhere* [laughs] in my impression of who Debbie is. So I don't have details. I mean, the details may not even be interesting to me. But what I've noticed is that she has a really lively, humorous way of looking at life, and she'd gone through cancer and she'd had this unusual surgery and these things, and she just was this effervescent person. *And I thought that was really special.*

There are several important elements that come out of this part of the elicitation. One is that Kendall is intentionally "looking for evidence to reinforce what I enjoy." She seeks it out, rather than waiting and hoping it reveals itself. And then, of course, she gets to enjoy whatever that is; noticing and enjoying feed each other. Second, if what is happening is not enjoyable, she will look for some small piece of what is going on that she *can* enjoy. And third, she stores away ("catalogues") what she finds enjoyable. This makes it easier to notice these details in future.

Secondary Strategies

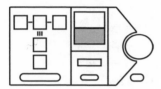

How could this happen? I was so careful. I picked the wrong play, the wrong director, the wrong cast... Where did I go right?!

Zero Mostel facing the disaster of success
in *The Producers*

Because real life is complex and unruly, an essential aspect of any competency is being able to respond usefully when things are *not* working out in the usual way. The person who has only her Primary Strategy upon which to rely—no matter how effective it usually is—is standing on thin experiential ice. A little too much sun, an errant crack, a duck landing nearby—anything not normally accounted for—and that person is sunk.

Being an exemplar of an ability means being consistently successful (excellent, effective, masterful) in a particular context; it does not mean that it is always easy to be successful. A true exemplar is not thrown by situational difficulties that her Primary Strategy is unable to handle. Instead, she has useful and effective backup strategies to deal with those difficult situations. These are her *Secondary Strategies*:

> Secondary Strategies are *the internal processes and external behaviors that are engaged when the Primary Strategy is ineffective.*

Depending upon the Ability and exemplar, there may be anything from none to dozens of Secondary Strategies. However, the range of possible Secondary Strategies can be usefully divided into three groups:

INSUFFICIENTLY WORKING

> *The Primary Strategy is not proving to be as effective as the exemplar would like.*

For instance, an executive coach's Primary Strategy of "Encourage the client to talk about his or her personal interests" may have produced some rapport with her client, but not as much as the coach needs. Consequently, she switches to a Secondary Strategy of "Reveal things about *your own* personal interests to the client."

NOT AT ALL WORKING

The Primary Strategy (and perhaps the Secondary
Strategy for "insufficiently working") are proving to
be completely ineffective.

In this instance the coach is gaining *no* rapport with her client (even though she has tried both "Encourage the client to talk about his or her personal interests" and "Reveal things about *your own* personal interests to the client"). When these approaches do not work, she shifts to another Secondary Strategy: "State directly that we are not in rapport, and ask questions to find out what might be in the way of our developing rapport."

CANNOT WORK

It does not seem possible to manifest the Ability.

This circumstance is a bit different from that of the previous two, both of which typically keep the exemplar moving toward the goal. But if the exemplar *does* get to the point of *does not seem possible*, then her Secondary Strategy will probably be one that allows her to let go of the goal (at least for the time being). For example, the executive coach recognizes that she cannot get rapport with her client. Her Secondary Strategy response to this situation might be to explain that she is not the appropriate person to coach the client, and she then helps the client find another coach.

These three categories of Secondary Strategies cover the range of real life situations for which we are likely to want or need effective, strategic alternatives.

Bear in mind that you may not find all three of these Secondary Strategies operating in your exemplar. For instance, when we modeled Lenny for his ability to keep himself on a diet regimen that controlled his diabetes, we found that he had no Secondary Strategy to cover the possibility that his Primary Strategy "was not working at all." Because of the dire consequences to his health, Lenny cannot let things get to the point of his diet strategy not working at all. And so he has only one Secondary Strategy, one that quickly gets him "back on track" if his usual strategy is not working well enough to keep him on his diet.[2] The Secondary Strategies you find for an Ability will depend upon the particular Ability you are modeling, and upon your exemplar.

Elicitation Questions for the Secondary Strategies

> **"What do you do when what you usually do is not working well enough?"**
>
> **"What do you do when what you usually do is not working at all?"**
>
> **"What do you do when what you usually do cannot work?"**

EXAMPLES

Q: What do you do when what you usually do to plan a celebration is not working well enough?

Adam: *I start again, with the imagining and so on, but this time I first think of some different aspect of who these attendees are; I bring out something that I was not considering before about who they are.* Often that will give me some new ideas.

Q: What do you do when your planning isn't working at all?

Adam: Well, then obviously I am missing something about these people, so *I will gather some more information; actually talk with a couple of them to find out what they love, hate, and so on.*

Q: What do you do when you determine that you will not be able to come up with a satisfactory plan?

Adam: *I do the best I can, go for the most people I can.* I hate doing that, though.

Q: What do you do when you're having difficulty in being patient with

---

[2] You will find a complete presentation and discussion of the Array for Lenny's ability to maintain a diet regimen in the Appendices.

a child?

Bridgit: That is a clear signal that *I need to reduce the size of the steps we're trying to take.*

Q: What do you do when you are not at all being patient?

Bridgit: Well, then *probably something is going on in my life that is more important at that time, something is occupying most of my attention. So I separate myself from the child and find out what is going on with me. Whatever it is, I take care of it so I can get back to the child."*

Q: What do you do when you realize that you are not going to be able to be patient with a child?

Bridgit: THAT does not happen.

Q: What do you do when how you usually approach designing a web site isn't working very well?

Claire: They're always pretty difficult, I find. I just keep working at moving things around, looking for possible misunderstandings, and so on until it's flowing.

Q: What do you do when you are not at all able to make a web site work?

Claire: *I try to think of other sites I have worked on or seen that were similar in content, in what they were trying to do. I look at some of those to see how I or someone else organized them.* And that usually gives me some clues I can take to the site that's giving me trouble.

Q: What do you do when you realize that it will not be possible to make a web site work?

Claire: This does happen once in awhile, and it is because there is something very flawed in the fundamental concept of the site. In those cases, *we have to go back to square one and look at what we want the site to do and be, and rebuild it from first principles.* That's the only way.

For Adam, situations in which his Primary Strategy is not working well enough, not working at all, or is not going to work are three, distinct situations, and he has different Secondary Strategies for handling each one.

Just because we can ask about each of these three possibilities, however, does not mean that they exist for the exemplar. Claire is an example of someone who does not have a distinct Secondary Strategy for "insufficiently working." For her there is only continuing to use her Primary Strategy, unless she hits the wall of being completely unable to make a web site work elegantly ("cannot work"). When that happens, she looks to other web sites for inspiration.

Bridgit does not have a Secondary Strategy for "cannot work." For her, "cannot work" is not a possibility; it is always possible to take even smaller steps, or to take care of whatever is distracting her from being with the child.

"Being Passionate About Something" – Eliciting the Secondary Strategies

Kendall does not seem to have—or need—Secondary Strategies for "Enjoy the Details" and for "Look for Deeper Meaning." For instance:

> David: So, when you search for that deeper meaning with Jaggy, does it ever happen that you can't find it?
>
> Kendall: I would have to guess that it does, but if it does happen it doesn't bother me. I mean, it's this . . . Maybe it doesn't happen. Maybe I am always finding it, because I'm really looking for evidence to support how much I enjoy this.
>
> David: Yeah, I believe that.
>
> Kendall: So I'm *finding* it…in ways that maybe other people wouldn't notice, but—It makes it pretty easy to be satisfied, by the way, you know, as a person, because I feel like I can be pretty well satisfied.

However, the key both to having details to enjoy and to finding deeper meaning is to "Pay Attention," and Kendall does have Secondary Strategies to support doing that:

"PAY ATTENTION" — NOT ENOUGH

> David: What do you do when you're… It must happen at times that you recognize that you are not as attentive as you

need or want to be. What do you do then?

Kendall: Well *first of all I notice it. I notice I'm thinking of other things, and I've missed something that my client said. So, I didn't hear them. That's an immediate cue— it only needs to happen one time and that's my cue, Okay, Kendall, I need to pay attention here. So the first part's just noticing that I stopped paying attention.*

David: And you do that by—you notice that you've *missed* something.

Kendall: I've *missed* something. "Oops, missed it." I must not have been paying attention. Because that's different to me than not understanding.

David: Right.

Kendall: So then *when that happens, I usually check my posture, my body position, and so, usually immediately—what I've noticed is that I've fallen out of that particular posture of being attentive. Which is more like this [demonstrating], with a pencil in my hand [laughs]. And, so, if I'm having trouble paying attention, I will pick up a pencil—make sure I have something in my hand, because that for me is an anchor—and I sit more forward, and I check in and make sure that I'm breathing.* And I'll start to—in my own, internal voice— I'll start to get after myself for not paying attention. I'll get critical of that. So I just tell myself, It's okay; pay attention [laughs]… Actually, no, you know what it is? *I go back to asking, because in my mind, part of paying attention for me is asking questions. I think a lot in questions. And so I, yeah, I go back to thinking— asking questions, either in my mind or verbally. It doesn't matter which it is.*

David: Uh huh. And, so…are these certain questions, or are there certain kinds of questions you ask, or is it, in order to get yourself back to being attentive—

Kendall: No. It's just—

David: It's just to start the actual—the effect *of* asking questions is to bring your attention back to the present.

Kendall: Right, right. Because when I've fallen out of paying attention, I'm usually not asking questions. I'm usually telling myself about other stuff.

"Missing something" is a signal that she probably has not been paying attention. She puts her body back into the posture that supports her being attentive: sitting forward, breathing, holding a certain amount of tension in her body and, as we learn here, finding something that serves as an anchor for paying attention. She also makes sure to resume asking questions. In addition to bringing her attention to the situation she is actually *in*, the answers to these questions are likely to generate details for her to notice and respond to (find deeper meaning in and enjoy).

"PAY ATTENTION" — NOT AT ALL

David: Does it ever happen that you're not—do you ever discover that, I'm not paying *any* attention. Or do you—

Kendall: Sometimes with clients, yes, on occasion.

David: What do you do then?

Kendall: I actually...*I ask a question [laughs]. It's different, though, because what I do is, I realize that in my own mind I'm useless to myself at that moment. It only happens if I'm really, really tired. And I just—I say less, I actually ask them less. But I ask them a more open-ended question that isn't designed so much to move them along.* It might be a question of—for example—of, What can I do that would be of most help to you right now? I often ask that question. *So it's just—for me it's an inner feeling of just letting go and giving up. It's like I, you know...they need to tell me because I don't know at this moment.*

David: Okay. Alright.

Kendall: And in my riding, if I'm really tired... For example, the other night, I was really tired and I thought, I wonder if I should even be riding, and I thought, well... Oh, I remember what question I asked myself. I asked, Do I really need to school my horse tonight or can I just ride? And I, I... I don't remember exactly the answer. I ended up kind of doing a combination of both and having a really good time. And feeling a tremendous amount of energy and thrill afterwards. Yeah.

Kendall recognizes that she can be too tired to pay attention. When she realizes that she does not have the energy she needs to pay attention, she accepts that, rather than try to ignore or overcome it. Instead, she asks a question that takes the form of, "What do I/you/we need to do right now?" This resets the frame for what *to* pay attention to. And, since it is a frame that takes into account the reality of her current state and situation, it is one in which she is likely to find details and nuances to appreciate (satisfying her Criterion of "Being Appreciative," which—as do all Criteria—continues to be important as long as she is in the relevant context).

"PAY ATTENTION" — CANNOT

David: Does it ever happen that you go, I *can't* pay attention? I just *can't* pay attention. I mean, there's a difference between I'm not *at all* paying attention and going I *can't*—

Kendall: *Yeah, well, that's what we just talked about when I said, You know what, I can't pay attention so I'm just going to turn it over to them.*

As we know from her previous explanation, she will shift her attention to something in which she can find something to appreciate. Kendall's Secondary Strategies go as far as "unable to pay attention"; that is, there is always a way to shift what is in the foreground of her attention. Therefore, the situation of "cannot" pay attention—in the sense of "it is not possible for attention to be paid"—does not really happen for her.

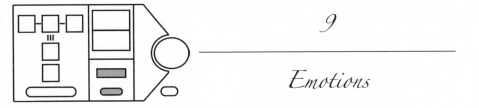

9

Emotions

We are capable of experiencing an enormous range of emotions. Our emotions are certainly experiences of the body, involving complicated patterns of hormonal, neuro-chemical, and central nervous system responses. However, no description based strictly on the emotionally intoxicating effects of hormones and neurotransmitters or on the mapping of central nervous system architecture can fully explain the range and qualities of our emotional experience.[1]

When talking about emotions it is useful to first be clear about the distinction between *emotions* and *feelings*. We often refer to our emotions as "feelings," but not everything we feel is an emotion. Touch a hot stove and you will feel pain and jerk your hand away; neither the sensation of pain nor the behavioral response of jerking your hand away is an emotion. Feeling angry with yourself for touching the hot stove *is* an emotion, however. Unlike sensations, which are reports about the state of your body at specific locales, emotions are reports about the state of you as a *whole system*. Whole-body sensations and feelings that coalesce into distinct patterns can become meaningful to us, and we call these distinctive, meaningful patterns *emotions*:

> Emotions are *meaningful, physiologically-based, whole-system states.*

Why do we need these whole system reports? Emotions are very efficient ways of organizing the whole organism (you) to respond effectively to those situations that require a full response. For instance, the response of your "animal body" to danger is immediate, extensive, and thorough: stillness, orienting toward the danger, crouching, accelerated heart beat, flood of adrenaline, tightening of viscera, and keen awareness. This whole body response we call *fear*, and is one of the six "universal" emotions—along with happiness, sadness, anger, surprise and disgust—that have been identified as characteristic of most mammals (and perhaps other animals as well).

---

[1] For research into the physiological basis of emotion, see Damasio (1994, 2000), Edelman (1992), LeDoux (1998), and Pert (1997).

To say that emotions are of the body is not to say that is *all* they are. In human beings emotions are also responses to *meaning*. Our ideas about the significance of things that exist and happen, both in the world around and within us, is as important a part of the flow of our lived—and emotional—world as are our sensory experiences. Human emotions are inextricably tied to meaning.

Imagine that your boss leans in through the door to your office and says, "I really appreciate your work on that report," then ducks back out. Perhaps you feel *proud*. That feeling of pride is your body instantly recognizing and weaving together the significance of countless contemporaneous threads: the fact that the boss is stopping by at all, the particular words he says, the genuine smile, the nod of his head, where he puts emphasis as he speaks, your memory of having worked hard on the report, your recent anxiety about where you stand with the boss, and so on. All of that comes together viscerally as an emotional experience called *proud*. An emotion is the weaving together of the concurrent threads of the moment—sights, sounds, sensations, words, memories and thoughts—into an experiential cloak. A slight change in the mix of the threads of the moment, however, and the emotion may very well come together differently. For instance, if you know that you have not put as much effort into the report as you should have, perhaps the emotional summing of the moment of being complimented by the boss would be one of *relief* (or perhaps *guilt*). Or if the boss instead says, "I really appreciate your work on that report," in a sarcastic tone of voice, your visceral mix might leave you feeling *shame* (or perhaps *resentment*).

As the office example suggests, because of our ability to make meaning, the range of human emotional experience extends far beyond the six universal emotions. We feel curiosity, desire, compassion, and love every bit as strongly as happiness, sadness, fear, anger, surprise, and disgust. In addition to happy, we can also have as distinct emotional experiences feeling thrilled, ecstatic, pleased, contented, joyful, cheerful, exultant, delighted, gratified, satisfied, excited, tickled, eager, energized, and so on. While all of these emotions may belong to the same "happy" family, each of them *feels* different. (If you doubt this, access them one at a time and notice how each one affects you.)

Different emotions not only feel different, each of them has different implications for how we respond as well. For instance, when we feel *satisfied* with a gift someone has given us, our response (what we think, say, and do) will probably be significantly different than if we feel *ecstatic* with the gift. That is obvious. What may not be as obvious, however, is that feeling very similar emotions—such as *satisfied* and *contented*—are also likely to lead to different responses. If you compare examples of feeling each of them, you will probably discover that they affect your experience and responses somewhat differently.

This means that a shift in emotions is not simply a shift in what you are feeling, but also in your perceptions, thinking, behavior…in the whole system that is you. When you feel sad, for instance, that feeling orients your attention toward what is awful in your world, triggers internal dialogue about how bad things are, decreases your sense of energy, slows your body movements, and so on. Then perhaps something *affecting* happens—a friend says a loving word, a child laughs, you recall a warm memory—and you begin to feel joyful. Now, suddenly, this feeling of joy is influencing what you attend to, say to yourself, sense in your body; now the dynamics of the whole system of your experience stabilize around *that* emotion. That is, until something else sufficiently affecting happens, stirring a different emotion and compelling the dynamics of the system to reform itself once again. Emotions, then, embody the sum total of the subjective significance of our perceptions and thoughts as they coalesce from moment to moment. And this embodying of significance often happens in the wink of an eye.

Signal Emotions

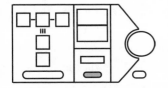

Suddenly you're afraid, and you don't know what you're afraid of. Did you ever get that feeling? Well, when I get it, the only thing that does any good is to jump into a cab and go to Tiffany's. Calms me down right away. The quietness and the proud look of it. Nothing very bad could happen to you there.

— Audrey Hepburn in *Breakfast at Tiffany's*

Emotions are our body's moment-to-moment summing up of our current experience. In doing this, our emotions are providing ongoing feedback on how well what we are doing (our internal processes and external behaviors) is satisfying our Criterion. Sometimes the effect of this emotional feedback is to signal the need to alter what we are doing.

For instance, a person whose project is going off track feels *frustrated* and, so, responds by reconsidering his priorities as a way of getting the project back on track; a person feels *wary* after a friend makes an uncaring comment, so she sits the friend down to talk it out, hoping to re-establish their mutual trust; a person feels *overwhelmed* by a huge task, so he breaks the task down into bite-sized pieces that he can successfully tackle (or he asks someone to help him with it; or he decides that the task isn't worth doing and, so, drops it). In each of these examples, the emotion signals a *need to respond*. That response is intended to change the situation so that the Criterion can be satisfied.

Emotions can also signal the *satisfaction* of Criteria. When the person pursuing the project recognizes that she is on track she may feel *happy*; the person who wants mutual trust may feel again *connected* to her friend when he shows regret for having hurt her; and the person facing the huge task may feel *confident* as he sees it progressing toward success. In these instances, their Emotions are signaling that their Criteria are being satisfied. In general, pleasant emotions do not signal the need to change what you are doing; they are signals that what you are doing (your Strategy) is working or has worked. They are telling you, "keep doing what you have been doing."

In all of these examples, emotions are serving as feedback signaling how well a Criterion is being satisfied:

> Signal Emotions are *moment-to-moment states that indicate whether or not—or to what degree—the Criterion is currently being satisfied.*

As we saw in the chapter on Strategies, an important part of excelling at any ability is having strategies for effectively responding when things go awry, as they occasionally will, no matter how effective the exemplar's Primary Operation may be. Signal Emotions often act as the prompt to engage one of the Secondary Operations. For example, an office manager who is a whiz at maintaining an organized office feels *calm* as long as his Primary Operation for dealing with incoming communiqués continues to work to satisfy his Criterion, "Maintain Order." Feeling *harried*, however, signals that his usual approach is not working and prompts him to shift to a Secondary Operation (perhaps to reassess and reset the categories he uses to sort incoming communiqués).

Naturally, the particular Signal Emotion you feel will vary depending on the situation and your personality. However, the range of Signal Emotions you experience can be usefully characterized according to whether your Criterion is being *exceeded*, *sufficiently satisfied*, *insufficiently satisfied*, or *violated*. For example, consider the person who wants "Mutual Trust" in relationships. Depending upon what is happening with respect to her Criterion in a particular situation, she might feel any of the following Signal Emotions:

WHEN "MUTUAL TRUST" IS:	SIGNAL EMOTION MAY BE:
EXCEEDED	*loving*
SUFFICIENTLY SATISFIED	*connected*
INSUFFICIENTLY SATISFIED	*wary*
VIOLATED	*afraid*

Typically, Signal Emotions are transient; they only continue until the Criterion is once again being sufficiently satisfied. For instance, the office manager will continue to feel *harried*, alerting him to the need to reset his sorting categories, until he again has "Order" and is in control of his office, in response to which he feels *relieved*. Because Signal Emotions change from moment to moment, they are typically the emotions of which we are most conscious.

Noticing Signal Emotions

There is usually no need to specify our exemplar's Signal Emotions. Signal Emotions serve to provide feedback signaling the need to either keep doing what you are doing or to change what you are doing, You will always have *some* emotional response as your Criterion is satisfied or not satisfied. As long as that emotional response serves to signal you that you need to either keep doing what you are doing or change what you are doing, it will work. In fact, most often you will find that if you are using the same Criterion as your exemplar you will naturally respond with Signal Emotions that are either the same or from the same family of emotions.

There are exceptions, however. It may be that a particular Signal Emotion is both unusual *and* important. Or it may be a common emotion, but so significant to the ability that it is important to note it. In either case, there is no elicitation question for the Signal Emotion. Because Signal Emotions tend to be those we notice, the exemplar will certainly offer them in her descriptions. When you step into her experience and try on her Signal Emotions, if any of them strike you as particularly worth noting, then note them.

EXAMPLES

Adam: When I'm having difficulty coming up with a plan that will really allow people to feel included, I feel very ***frustrated***.

Bridgit: I was working with a 7-year-old yesterday, and finally she was able to do subtraction for the first time and I was ***thrilled!***

Claire: Sometimes I realize I am feeling ***deeply concerned***—like you would feel for someone in possible danger—and when I do I know I am looking at a site that is fundamentally flawed.

We have examples of Signal Emotions from both Adam and from Bridgit, but neither of them is probably worth noting in models of their abilities. Most of us would naturally feel *frustrated* (or an emotion akin to it, such as *aggravated* or *determined*) when having difficulty coming up with an "inclusive plan" for a celebration. Similarly, Bridgit's *thrilled* (or, perhaps, *delighted* or *deeply pleased*) is something any of us is likely to feel if we care about "Movement," and have been working with a child who has "finally moved!"

Claire's Signal Emotion, however, may be worth including in her model. Feeling *deeply concerned* is not what we might expect when trying to bring "Elegance" to a website. The intensity of this Signal Emotion alerts her to the fact that she is dealing with a web site that needs more drastic measures than she had expected, and impels her to use one of her Secondary Strategies (e.g. "Go back to square one and look at what we want the site to do and be, and rebuild it from first principles").

Sustaining Emotions

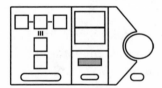

Our living conditions were abysmal, yet I had never been happier. We slept on broken bunks or on the ground under the stars. If it rained, we got wet. Our tools consisted of picks, axes and shovels. An older woman among us—she was in her sixties—recalled tales of having done similar work after World War I in 1918. She made us feel blessed for the little we did have.

— Elisabeth Kübler-Ross in *The Wheel of Life*

We all know the difference an ongoing emotional state ("mood") can make in how the day goes. Wake up on the proverbial wrong side of the bed and everything seems to go wrong: You huddle beneath a gray sky and chilling rain as you reluctantly make your way to work, where an ominous swamp of papers awaits you. You plunge in and deal with those papers, but you are vexed again and again by their many stupid errors. A co-worker pops in to offer a joke, but you impatiently wave him away. You check the clock and are disappointed to find that there are still *hours* left before you can escape to lunch. And so it goes…

Until the next day, when you unaccountably wake up on the "right" side of the bed. It is again gray and rainy, but you enjoy the smell of it and think how good this will be for a spectacular spring flower bloom. At work, the pile of papers on your desk is a challenge that you eagerly tackle. There are still as many errors in the papers as yesterday, but today you take pride in finding and correcting them. Your co-worker dares to try another joke and you laugh heartily, then cheerfully shoo him out so you can get your work done before lunch.

As these examples illustrate, unlike the transient Signal Emotions, emotions can also persist in the background of our experience, where they generally affect how we respond to almost everything. We call this persistent and pervasive background emotion the *Sustaining Emotion*:

> The Sustaining Emotion is *a background state that*
> *helps keep the person actively engaged in manifesting*
> *the Ability.*

Unlike Signal Emotions, the Sustaining Emotion is *not* providing ongoing feedback on whether or not the Criterion is being satisfied. Instead, the Sustaining Emotion is setting an emotional environment that supports the continuing pursuit of the Criterion and the use of the Strategies that make up the Ability.

You can think of the Sustaining Emotion as a way of holding the structural distinctions that are important in a particular context. Another way to put it is that the Sustaining Emotion is holding *in the body* at least some of the essential concerns and relationships that are operating in the beliefs and strategies of the Ability. The result of this alignment is greater congruence in thought and action, as well as making it easier to *continue* operating out of the beliefs and strategies of the Ability. Three examples:

* An acquaintance of ours is devoted to solving crossword puzzles, and feels *challenged* when doing them. Feeling challenged generates a sense that there is something he wants to and *can* overcome, even though it will be difficult. Feeling challenged keeps him engaged in solving the puzzle, even when he finds himself reading the last clue and still has not filled in a single square! Not surprisingly, if he begins a crossword puzzle that is too easy—sapping his feeling of being *challenged*—he soon sets

it aside.

* Another acquaintance is often in the position of leading teams in her company. When in that context, her Sustaining Emotion is that of feeling *responsible*. Feeling responsible, she recognizes there are things that need to be done, she is capable of doing them, and they are hers to do. And so she works diligently with the group, with plenty of oversight on their activities (some say too much), never shirks a task in service of the team, and is quick to admit her lapses when she drops one of the balls.[2]

* A colleague of ours is a master at tracking down information. He is clever, bold, and relentless in pursuing it, and almost always successful. When on the trail of his quarry, his Sustaining Emotion is *pleasant anticipation*, the effect of which is to hold out the promise that he is inexorably moving toward something that will be very satisfying. Thus, despite going down many blind alleys and facing many locked doors, he persists, fueled by the pleasant anticipation of what will be found around the next corner.

The ongoing, background nature of Sustaining Emotions means that they often go unnoticed by the exemplar. When you first put on a sock you are very aware of the sensations of it encasing your foot and constricting your calf. But soon you no longer notice the sock—that is, until the top of the sock slips down to your ankle. What grabs our attention is change. (As we noted earlier, the emotions we are most aware of are our frequently shifting Signal Emotions.) When it comes to elicitation, this means that Sustaining Emotions may not be as readily accessible or as easily put into words as the other elements of experience.

Stepping-in provides a way to test whether an emotion your exemplar describes is likely to be her Sustaining Emotion. If you find that the emotion needs to be repeatedly prompted in order to keep it in experience, then it is probably not a Sustaining Emotion. Also, a Sustaining Emotion can be held or maintained in experience regardless of whether the Criterion is being satisfied, not satisfied, exceeded, or violated.

---

[2] Everyone would agree that, "*of course* she is responsible for the team—she's a manager." But that is a performance expectation of her *role*. Any person in her role would be responsible for team performance. However, that person might not *feel* responsible, but instead feel *ambitious*, or *careful*, or *driven*, each of which would dramatically affect how this person fulfilled their responsibility to lead the team.

Elicitation Questions for the Sustaining Emotion

> **"What is the background feeling that keeps you engaged in [Ability]?"**
>
> — or —
>
> **"When you are [Ability], what emotion is always operating in the background of your experience to help *keep* you [Ability]?"**

EXAMPLES

Q: What is the background feeling that *keeps* you engaged in planning a celebration?

Adam: Well, through the entire process it's almost as though it is already happening. I see how great it will be, and I'm feeling this sense of *excitement* about what the celebration can be.

Q: When you are being patient with a child, what emotion is always operating in the background of your experience to help *keep* you being patient?

Bridgit: *Love*. I'm just *loving* that child the whole time.

Q: When you are designing an interface for a website, what emotion is always operating in the background of your experience that helps *keep* you working at it?

Claire: It's a feeling of "I'm just going to do it somehow," you know? It's a challenge, I feel *challenged*.

As soon as you step into the contexts of these three Abilities the importance of their Sustaining Emotions in supporting the Ability becomes evident. When we feel *excitement* we are eagerly looking forward to something that we expect to happen; what could be better than that for planning a celebration? When we feel *loving* we are connected to, and accepting of, another person as she or he is; this is a perfect support for being patient with children. And when we feel *challenged* we are determined to overcome some difficulty; this is a useful emotion to feel when a flawed website interface needs time and effort to be turned into something elegant.

A useful way to test whether or not a particular emotion is a Sustaining Emotion for your exemplar is to ask her if she can continue to manifest her Ability even when that emotion is no longer there. If she can congruently manifest her Ability (that is, she is not simply going through the motions) even when she is not feeling that particular emotion, then it is almost certainly not a Sustaining Emotion. (Instead, it is probably a Signal Emotion.) However, if when the emotion goes away, so does the congruent manifestation of her ability, then that emotion probably *is* a Sustaining Emotion.

"Being Passionate About Something" – Eliciting the Sustaining Emotion

David: When you are feeling passionate, being passionate—with your horses, with your husband, with your clients—being passionate...what are you *feeling*, that is, what emotion is kind of always operating in the background of your experience that kind of helps *keep* you there in that passionate experience?

Kendall: *My first thought was "excitement."* And by the way, when you said "clients," with my business, it's also about the products that I create. And I feel just as passionate about those as I do about working with people. And I'm just thrilled with the products that I've created, and I'm thrilled because they help people. People find them really helpful. They send me emails and they call and tell me, so it feeds that passion for wanting to do more.

David: So you're feeling excited.

Kendall: *Excited. Yeah. And then "grateful."*

David: Yeah—

Kendall: *Really grateful.*

David: That's one I was wondering about, because, you remember when we were first talking early on—

Kendall: *Oh I remember. And the word "grateful" comes up for me in my own mind's...ear so often. But when you asked the question, though, the first word was "excited," and then the second one would be "grateful."*

David: Do they switch back and forth? Does it seem like they're both kind of *there?*—

Kendall: It's like I'm really excited and *"Man*, am I grateful I can be this excited!" I'm grateful that I have so much enjoyment in my life.

David: I see.

Kendall: ***I'm grateful about that [points to "excited" on flipchart].***

David: About that. I see.

Kendall: ***Which makes me really excited [inscribes a circle between "excited" and "grateful," and laughs] A little loop there that goes on.***

David: Ah hah! Got it.

Feeling "thrilled" (really enjoying what *is happening* or *has just happened*) is something Kendall feels in response to recognizing that what she has produced is appreciated by her clients, and is a Signal Emotion.

Kendall has two Sustaining Emotions—"excited" and "grateful"—that are more or less constantly feeding each other in the background of her experience. Feeling *excited* sets her to expect something wonderful. (And, as she says elsewhere during the elicitation, "if you're looking for something, you tend to find it.") Because she is looking for small things (details), she finds them easily and much of the time and, so, can feel *grateful* much of the time that she gets to be *excited*.

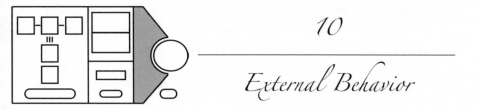

10

External Behavior

> One may have a blazing hearth in one's soul,
> and yet no one ever comes to sit by it.
> — Vincent van Gogh

Our behaviors are generally so evident to us, so much what we notice and talk about, that we often do not accord them the level of regard they deserve. And that is this: In terms of the external world, our thoughts and feelings mean nothing; our behaviors, however, mean everything. The only way the external world can know the opinions, discoveries, ideas, visions, and feelings stirring inside the vast world of your experience is through what you do, through your expressions, and through what you say and how you say it. It is through behavior that you have an impact on the world, and it is through behavior that the world knows you. Your *external behavior* is the interface between you and the world.

External behavior includes behaviors as obvious as running around the room and as subtle as leaning slightly forward. They can be as simple as raising an eyebrow, or as complex as tying a shoe lace. Speaking is also external behavior; saying to someone, "I would like to give my opinion," is a different behavior—and has a different effect—than saying, "I'm going to tell you the way it is." Even the tonality with which things are said is external behavior. Saying, "I'm going to tell you the way it is," in a squeaky and hesitant voice is a different behavioral expression than saying the same thing in a slow and resonant voice. External behavior, then, encompasses everything that we do on the outside: that is, anything that can be seen or heard by someone else. When modeling, we are not interested in all behaviors, however, but only those that are *necessary* for a particular ability to work:

> External Behaviors are *those behaviors (movements,*
> *facial expressions, verbalizations and voice tonalities)*
> *that are significant in manifesting an Ability.*

Because External Behavior is the interface, it is understandable that our initial inclination might be to focus our modeling on behavior. After all, ultimately we are interested in manifesting the exemplar's behavior. That is where the action is, and those actions make possible the outcomes we hope to attain by making her Ability our own. Nevertheless, there are three very good reasons to instead focus our attention on the beliefs, strategies, and emotions operating in the exemplar:

ACCESS — For most human abilities, merely mimicking External Behavior will not give us sufficient access to *essential* internal processes. Being able to forgive someone, debugging computer programs, or appreciating modern art are all examples of abilities for which patterns of belief and thinking are essential. (Holding out your hand to someone who has wronged you will not necessarily create the empathy needed to *actually* forgive that person; but *feeling* empathy *is* likely to make it easy and natural to hold out your hand to him.)

RELIABILITY — Experience comes as a package. Behaviors do not operate in spite of thoughts, thoughts in spite of feelings, feelings in spite of beliefs. The dynamic combining of all of these elements of experience *is* the Ability. If an Ability is to be reliable—that is, we can be sure of it operating effectively—there needs to be an internal structure of experience that supports and *naturally* manifests the necessary External Behaviors.

DEPTH —If you try to manifest an Ability solely through using its External Behaviors, you become an automaton, and your competence is brittle, precarious, and easily overwhelmed. Because of the unpredictability of real life, *true* competency is demonstrated when a person can continue to effectively manifest an Ability even as the demands of the situation change. This flexibility of response comes from the internal processes which generate the exemplar's External Behavior as she responds to the demands of the moment.

The Beliefs, Strategies, and Emotions establish perceptions, intentions and states that naturally give rise to most of the External Behaviors needed to manifest the Ability. For instance, if you believe that it is important to have a "neat" environment, you will naturally put things away where they belong; if, when making choices, your thinking involves "getting direct answers to your questions," you will naturally ask questions when faced with a choice; if you are feeling "loving" toward someone, your facial expression will naturally be relaxed, and your voice tonality and touch naturally softer. Because much of External Behavior is the natural result of internal processes, it is not necessary to catalogue all of the exemplar's behaviors in order to ensure that they will be available and operating in you when you use her model.

However, there may be important External Behaviors that cannot be counted on to emerge automatically. A woodworker who exhales as he glides his chisel forward; or a teacher who spreads her arms wide and inclines her head as she asks her student to settle down; or a negotiator whose voice tonality becomes deep and smooth when speaking of someone's grievances, are all examples of distinctive External Behaviors that we might not automatically manifest ourselves unless we were told to do them. The External Behaviors we want to be sure to include in our model, then, are those that are both essential *and* we are not likely to do as a natural consequence of operating out of the exemplar's internal structure.

Elicitation Question for the External Behavior

The best way of identifying significant External Behaviors is by observing the exemplar in action, manifesting her Ability. As we discussed in Chapter 3 (*The Process*), it is important to see your exemplar in action, manifesting her ability either with others or with you. In this way, you can directly see the behaviors and hear the words and voice tonalities that she either takes for granted or of which she is unconscious. However, during elicitation you can also ask:

"What are you doing on the outside—in your behavior—that is essential to manifesting [Ability]?"

EXAMPLES
_____

    Q: What are you doing on the outside—in your behavior—that is essential to planning a successful celebration?

Adam: I can't think of anything in particular. (Observing him make such a plan, though, we see that before each time he imagines being an attendee, he *takes a deep breath and settles his shoulders.*)

    Q: What are you doing on the outside—in your behavior—that

is essential to being patient with a child who is learning?

Bridgit: *I never sit above or below the child; always on the same level. And I speak to her directly, like she was another, intelligent adult, even if I am using a simpler vocabulary.*

Q: What are you doing on the outside—in your behavior—that is essential to designing an easy-to-use web site?

Claire: Well, I look at the screen, move the mouse around and try buttons and links, of course. But I don't think those things are what you mean by "essential." Oh, I growl with disgust sometimes, too!

Bridgit is quite aware of some of her significant behavior and can describe it directly. Claire is also aware of her behavior and can describe it, but we do not note it as External Behavior because "looking at the screen, moving the mouse around, etc." are behaviors that anyone engaged in that context would naturally do. By contrast, "Growling with disgust" is not something most people would automatically do in that context. But is it relevant to manifesting the Ability to design an easy-to-use web site? If not, then we do not note it.

Unlike Bridgit, Adam is not aware that any of his external behavior is essential to his ability. But when we observe him in action, we notice that he does have some distinctive External Behaviors: He takes a deep breath and settles his shoulders each time he begins his planning. When we step into trying on his ability with those same External Behaviors, we notice that it seems to help us clear our minds, so we can more accurately imagine the experiences of the attendees. When we feed this observation back to Adam, it allows him to be aware of *his* own experience and he confirms that the deep breath and settling of his shoulders has the same effect on him, too.

"Being Passionate About Something" – Eliciting the External Behavior

David: When you are being passionate—in being passionate— what are you doing on the outside, what are you doing in your external behavior…what are you doing that the rest of the world would see or hear that is *significant* in terms of being passionate?

Kendall: I know they hear the *energy in my voice*, because I've had a lot of people comment on that. Um…

David: Are you *doing* anything in your external behavior that
          helps make it possible to be—

Kendall: ***Well I actually do the activities***, you know. I mean, I
          work on my business. So I don't just think about work-
          ing on my business. *I think about it and then I put those
          thoughts into action. I actually do them.* You know, I
          could think about learning photography and doing some
          photography. I'm not passionate about it, I'm not putting
          those thoughts into action. Because it's not really satisfying.
          So, from a big picture level, *I'm actually putting
          thought into action. I'm taking action. And that action
          can be many—there's all different kinds of action, but
          I'm physically taking action; picking up the telephone,
          or sending an email, or designing a training piece.*

David: Or telling somebody that you just noticed something
          about them to appreciate.

Kendall: *Or telling them, Yeah. Absolutely. Right. Yes… And
          actually, I physically—I really am very physically
          aware of looking for…making sure I've attended to
          demonstrating that appreciation.* So, I have been known
          to—and I'll appreciate a difficult situation. Somebody
          putting their honesty and their heart into working
          through a difficult situation, I really appreciate. And I'll
          tell them that, say, "This is really difficult and I really
          appreciate you being willing to work this through." And
          I've been known to get off the phone and, on occasion,
          call them back—whether it's a family member or a
          friend or a client—call them back and say, "You know, I
          just wanted to let you know." Yeah. *And that's very
          much putting thought into action, because I think a lot
          of people would just say, Oh, it's okay. And I've tried
          that, tried doing that, and ach, I wouldn't be able to
          sleep that night. I try it and it's…unh uh, doesn't work.*
          So people are noticing action, they're noticing physical
          movement, and I—yeah, they're noticing physical
          movement, and they're noticing the output of my
          physical movement. So they notice me riding. My
          neighbors all notice me riding five or six days a week.
          You know, classes being scheduled through the internet,

or whatever it is I'm taking action on. *That's* what people are seeing. ***And they're hearing in my voice, the energy.*** They always say, "Kendall, you're *so* enthusiastic about what you're doing." I say, "Oh, I *love* what I do."

[FROM ELICITATION OF THE EVIDENCE]

Kendall: It's quite a lot of feeling, actually, and I feel filled up inside, in my upper body...***and I have a sense of coming forward—I don't know that I could really appreciate something if I was slouching and leaning back...I can't imagine doing that...***

[FROM ELICITATION OF THE STRATEGY]

Kendall: ***I'm sitting forward***—which is actually not how—***I'm sitting forward, not leaning back . There's probably a certain amount of tension in my body of readiness.***

Kendall's ability to be passionate about something is built around her being appreciative. As she points out above, people can be appreciative without necessarily expressing that in their behavior. Kendall makes sure to somehow express behaviorally what she is appreciating: "I really am very physically aware of looking for...making sure I've attended to demonstrating that appreciation." Since the three contexts in which she is passionate all involve other people (her horse, Jaggy, is definitely a person to her), her behavior naturally involves letting them know what she is appreciating about them.

Expressing appreciation is a specific (and essential) instance of a more general External Behavior, which is, "I put those thoughts into action. I actually do them." For Kendall, being passionate about something means turning her thoughts (regarding what she is passionate about) into action. It is easy to see how this behavior is essential to the Ability. As soon as you somehow express or act on your appreciation of something, your experience changes; you *engage* with whatever it is that you are appreciating. The sense of separation dissolves and suddenly you are connected *to* that something. This being *engaged with* is an essential quality of being passionate about something.

Kendall's first answer about her External Behavior is that there is "energy in my voice." Even though this is obviously a characteristic behavior, we do not set it down in the model as External Behavior because it is something that naturally manifests itself in most anyone who is being passionate about something. Her leaning forward and holding a body tension of readiness (described at other times during the elicitation) may also be behavior that naturally emerges when anyone is being passionate about something. However, because its effect on our experience is *so* significant, and because Kendall uses it both as a way to know she is not paying attention *and* as something to *do* to pay attention, we felt that it is important to explicitly include "leaning forward" and "tension of readiness" in the model.

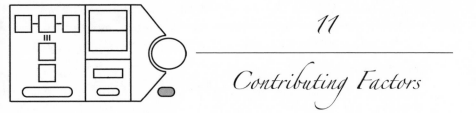

11

Contributing Factors

When we specify the Ability we want to model, we are establishing certain contextual boundaries in the world of the exemplar's experience. This is necessary if we want to avoid getting lost in the layered complexity of human experience. In drawing our boundaries we are endeavoring to fence in those elements of experience that are essential to the exemplar's Ability. This does not mean that everything else that gets fenced out is irrelevant or not useful. Some of these other abilities, skills, information, tools, or environmental conditions may contribute in significant ways to the ability. We call these *Contributing Factors*:

> Contributing Factors are *abilities, prerequisites, preparations, conditions, or considerations outside of the Array that significantly support the Ability.*

Contributing Factors make a significant difference in effectively manifesting an Ability *and* they are *outside* of the Array. They are not necessary parts of the structure of the Ability itself. For instance, suppose that someone who has the ability to be well-prepared for exams remarks that getting plenty of rest makes that preparation easier, and even more effective. When we explore other examples of her preparation for tests, however, we discover that getting a lot of rest is not an *essential* aspect of how she actually studies for an exam; she has found that rest can contribute to the outcome of being prepared for the test, but it does not determine the outcome. For her, then, getting rest is a Contributing Factor. (If instead we had found that getting plenty of rest is a necessary element in all of her examples of preparing for tests, we would then put it *inside* the Array in some form.) Almost anything can constitute a Contributing Factor:

Information: You can acquire a master craftsman's ability to design furniture, but knowing the strengths and finishing characteristics of various woods could contribute significantly to your design work.

Other abilities: The ability to create interesting fictional characters might be enhanced by the ability to empathize with strangers.

Objects and environments: Some negotiators who specialize in resolving acrimonious disputes find it helpful to conduct the negotiation in an environment that conveys a sense of their power, and so they make sure to have a large desk, Mont Blanc pens, photographs of themselves with prominent people, and so on.

If a Contributing Factor is itself an ability (for instance, "being able to empathize") then it, too, can be modeled and added to your repertoire (if you do not already have it), making you that much more effective in manifesting the primary ability in which you are interested.

Noticing Contributing Factors

Contributing Factors capture something that both operates outside of the Array itself, and makes a significant difference in our effectively manifesting the ability. Of course, everything "outside the Array" is everything but the Array. So we do not use an elicitation question for Contributing Factors, since such a question would invite being swamped by the sea of possibilities. Instead—like Supporting Beliefs and Signal Emotions—we note Contributing Factors when they arise.

EXAMPLES

Adam: It's true that *I do a lot of reading—magazine articles, books, newspaper articles—about what is going on in society, about the different generations, what they are into, thinking, dealing with, the different industries, and so on.* You have to be tuned in.

Bridgit: *I have a special room set aside for working with the children. And in there, everything is on their scale—not childish—just on their scale.*

Claire: *I do spend a lot of time just surfing around on the web, to see what's out there.* Mostly it is annoying, but once in awhile you find some little piece that's brilliant, that's worth, well, stealing the idea. You have to stay up on what is out there.

In each of these cases, we could operate out of the exemplars' Arrays *without* adopting their Contributing Factors. But it is easy to imagine that our effectiveness might be enhanced if we do use them: if we keep current on what is going on in the various segments of society, our ability to imagine celebration attendees will be freed from being trapped within the scope of whatever era we already know; having a room like the one Bridgit uses may reduce some of the barriers to comfort and trust, making the work with the children go easier; and surfing the net like Claire helps ensure that the elegant solutions we bring to our web site designs are contemporary, something that is important in the fast-changing world of the internet.

"Being Passionate About Something" – Contributing Factors

David: Is there anything I didn't ask you about that I ought to have?

Kendall: Didn't ask me about…I think one thing I made a slight comment on just a moment ago that, in thinking about this session today, that I think is very important is that, for me, *I'm not willing to live without passion in my life.* It's just not, um—it's beyond not okay. [laughs] And, so, there have been times in my life where I certainly had a dip in that, or there wasn't enough of it in my life…and I didn't tolerate it for very long. And it's not that I forced finding something artificially that I could be passionate about, but I actually became passionate about finding something I was passionate about. I approached them with the same amount of energy. So it's—I think that's really important, that level—that high water mark—has to stay there.

David: Now, you said something very interesting I just want to follow up on. "I'm not willing to live without passion in my life"—

Kendall: Nope.

David: And so you—as I understand it—you started looking for that which you could be passionate about.

Kendall: And looking for the things in my life that were stealing that energy or sucking that energy away, and getting rid of them.

Kendall's unwillingness to live without passion in her life is obviously significant in her being passionate about something. As she points out, she is going to be passionate about *something*, even if it is being passionate about the search for something to be passionate about. It is also clear that this determination to have passion is not necessary to being passionate. That is, a person does not necessarily need to be looking for passion to be swept into being passionate about something.

However, "not being willing to live without passion in my life" brings great intensity to being passionate. It also makes one protective of that passion. As Kendall says, she was "looking for the things in my life that were stealing that energy or sucking that energy away, and getting rid of them." For these reasons, it seems to us worth including "I'm not willing to live without passion in my life" in the model as a Contributing Factor.

12

Creating the Initial Array

Now you are no longer directly engaged with your exemplar and the intricacies of elicitation. Now you are free to be alone with the elements of experience you have discovered and to create the initial Array. To be "creating" the initial Array means to be at the stage in which you make sure you have captured in the Array those sentences and phrases of your exemplar that *work* to manifest the Ability.

Much of the Array may already be in place, of course. Because you were stepping in and trying on the various elements of experience as you gathered information, you have already recorded most of what is relevant to the Ability. Still, if you are like us, much of the information you have is in the form of scraps of comments, scribbled phrases, redundancies, and scattered notes joined by arrows. In addition, you may have some strong impressions from your experience with your exemplar that are not yet down on the page.

On the next pages you will find our initial Array for Kendall's ability to be passionate about something. We will use her Array as an example of the kinds of considerations that go into this stage of forming the model. This will also give us an opportunity to let you in on the thinking we were actually doing as we went through the process of creating her initial Array.

Creating the initial Array involves checking that you have the elements of experience in the correct boxes. Being particular about where things go is important because *where* you put them in the Array tells us a lot about *what* function a particular element serves in our experience, and how it systemically relates to other elements. For instance, suppose in modeling a business manager we found out that it is important to her to "connect with people" and to "succeed." Just which is the Criterion and which is the Prime Motivator? That is, how do these two concerns relate to one another? "Connecting with people *leads to* Success" generates a set of choices and behaviors that is very different from those generated by "Success *leads to* Connecting with people."

You create the initial Array in much the same way that you did the elicitation. That is, you test the significance of the bits of description you have by taking them on in your own experience and imagine manifesting the

THE INITIAL ARRAY FOR KENDALL

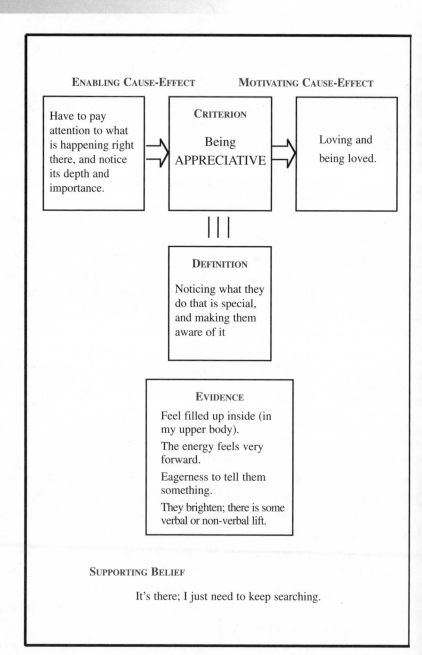

ENABLING CAUSE-EFFECT   MOTIVATING CAUSE-EFFECT

Have to pay attention to what is happening right there, and notice its depth and importance.

CRITERION

Being APPRECIATIVE

Loving and being loved.

DEFINITION

Noticing what they do that is special, and making them aware of it

EVIDENCE

Feel filled up inside (in my upper body).

The energy feels very forward.

Eagerness to tell them something.

They brighten; there is some verbal or non-verbal lift.

SUPPORTING BELIEF

It's there; I just need to keep searching.

PRIMARY STRATEGY

PAY ATTENTION

- Sit upright, with forward energy and the tension of readiness.
- Hold the Big Picture.
- Ask yourself questions that draw out the details and nuances of what you are attending to.
- Be flexible in terms of what to pursue.

ENJOY DETAILS

Enjoy the details of what you are noticing ⟳ Notice the details of what you are enjoying

- Catalogue and store what you are appreciating so it more easily comes to your attention in the future.

LOOK FOR DEEPER MEANING

Search details and nuances for clues to what is meaningful.
- Notice anything that is different or new.
- Anything that is a forward movement (a step in alignment with where you/they want to go), or a stretch (able to do something you/they were not able to do before) is meaningful.
- Deepen that meaning by discovering...
    "How is this important?"
    "What does it mean?"
    ...in relation to the Big Picture.

SECONDARY STRATEGIES

When you are not as attentive as you would like to be:
1. Notice that you've missed something.
2. Check posture (forward energy) and breathing.
3. Go back to asking questions (either in your mind or verbally).

When you are not at all attentive:
(This may happen when you are really tired.) Ask an open-ended question, such as "What can I do that would be of most help to you right now?"

SUSTAINING EMOTION

Excited / Grateful (blessed and lucky) ⟳

EXTERNAL BEHAVIOR

Body held upright, and leaning forward.

ABILITY

BEING PASSIONATE ABOUT SOMETHING:

Caring so deeply about something that you engage in it eagerly and often, and in many different ways.

I actually do the activities; I put my thoughts into action.

Tell people what I am appreciating.

CONTRIBUTING FACTORS

I know what I enjoy.

I'm not willing to live without passion in my life.

Ability. When you do that, notice how each element affects your experience; what does it seem to be *doing* in your experience? Going back to our manager example, for instance, when you try emulating her ability to manage people while holding "Success" as your Criterion, you find out that it does not work (as the Criterion it leads you to ignore your employees' emotional responses). "Connecting with people," however, *does* work as the Criterion; "Success" seems instead to be what is *motivating* your efforts to connect with people.

This is a good time to remember that these bits of description *carry* the experiential structures. This means that we need to be careful about the words we use in the Array. Because our goal in creating the initial Array is to accurately capture the *exemplar's* description of the patterns that are operating in her experience and behavior, we want to be sure to use her descriptions; those are the words and phrases that are expressive of the structure of her experience.

"Being Passionate About Something" — *The Initial Array*

THE BELIEF TEMPLATE

CRITERION

During the elicitation, our Belief Template for Kendall had "Appreciative" as her Criterion. Some criteria represent an end point, such as when you are looking for a restaurant that has a "friendly atmosphere"; once you have found that restaurant you are done with the "friendly atmosphere" criterion. Other criteria operate as ongoing evaluations that we are continually trying to satisfy. Kendall's Criterion is of this kind. She is never done with appreciating when she is engaged in helping others, being with her horse, or being with her husband; it is continually the primary focus of her attention. So, **"Being Appreciative"** more correctly conveys the ongoing quality of her Criterion. (In fact, in reviewing the elicitation, we recognized that she always referred to her Criterion as *"being* appreciative.")

DEFINITION

Often the first version of the Definition in the elicitation includes details that are particular to the exemplar's home example (the main example used during the elicitation). The elicitation of Kendall's Definition of "Being Appreciative" came from her home example of being passionate about her work: *"Notice the detailed things that they do that are special, and telling them about it."* In that context, she recognized that she was "noticing details" and "telling them [clients]" what she noticed.

That first version of the Definition naturally set a frame for our thinking when we then checked it against the other two examples of being passionate (riding and her relationship with her husband). Consequently, during the elicitation we saw only that this definition fit those examples, as well. But later, after the elicitation, we looked again at the examples of being passionate about horseback riding and her relationship with her husband, and recognized two things. First, in all three contexts she is noticing details, but "details" itself does not cover the entire range of what she is actually noticing; she is noticing something **"special they do."** Second, *telling* them about what she is noticing is only one of the ways she can let others (clients, her horse, her husband, herself) know what she is noticing. So in order to have a Definition that covered the true range of her experience, it needed to be broadened to become, **"making them aware of it."**

We also changed "notice" to "notic*ing*" to reflect the ongoing nature of the Criterion, "Being Appreciative." (Because the Criterion is the label for the experience described in the Definition—two sides of the same experiential coin—they will be consistent with each other.) So the Definition becomes, **"Noticing what they do that is special, and making them aware of it."**

EVIDENCE

In the original Template we wrote down, "Feel filled up in my upper body." This seemed a little ambiguous to us when we tried it on; feeling "filled up" could take us to feeling "stuffed," or "overwhelmed," and so on. What Kendall actually first said was "*I feel filled up inside*." This works much better. When we say "I feel filled up *inside*," it is clear that we are not talking about food, for instance, but about an emotional state. So this piece of the Evidence became **"Feel filled up inside (in my upper body)."**

"Leaning forward" was a second piece of Evidence. However, when we went back and listened again to how Kendall described how she knows she is being appreciative, we recognized that we had made this piece of Evidence more behavioral than she apparently experiences it:

Kendall: …and I have *a sense of coming forward*—I don't
know that I could really appreciate something if I was
slouching and leaning back…I can't imagine doing
that—so it feels somehow *the energy feels very forward*
and my body feels filled up…

When we stepped into her Ability, it was clear that "leaning forward" is a frequent behavioral expression of experiencing "forward energy." But it seemed to us that it is the "feeling forward energy" that is significant. In whatever way it may express itself behaviorally, it is experiencing that energy that really means to Kendall "I am being appreciative." So we changed this piece of Evidence to, **"The energy feels very 'forward.'"**

"They 'brighten'; there is a 'lift' in them." In reviewing the elicitation, however, we find that Kendall was explicit that the "lift" she is looking for can be evident in what they say or do:

Kendall: They have to brighten somehow. *They either have to say
something or have a look on their fac*e…I'm thinking of
clients, my horse, my husband…*they have to have some
verbal or non-verbal…lift to them*.

This seemed an important addition, so we changed the Evidence to, "They 'brighten'; there is some verbal or non-verbal 'lift.'"

ENABLING CAUSE-EFFECT

During the elicitation, we wrote down, "Have to pay attention to what is happening right there that is meaningful." When we reviewed the Belief Template with Kendall during the elicitation, however, she recognized that there was something that needed to be added:

> Kendall: ...you have to notice sometimes the **_meaning under-neath_** what they've said... [...] So it's really—I keep thinking of the word **_"depth."_** **_It's noticing the depth and importance of what just happened._**

We recognized that including Kendall's elaboration of "meaningful" helped us better identify *what* is meaningful and important to notice. The Enabling Cause-Effect became, **"Have to pay attention to what is happening right there, and notice its depth and importance."**

 MOTIVATING CAUSE-EFFECT

We found nothing that needed to be changed in capturing Kendall's Motivating Cause-Effect, and so we included it in the initial Array just as it came out in the elicitation: **"Loving and being loved."**

 SUPPORTING BELIEF

As we reviewed the elicitation with Kendall, one thing that jumped out at us as a possible Supporting Belief was her statement, **"It's there; I just need to keep searching."** When we held that belief as we experimented with stepping into being passionate about something, we found that it made a significant difference in our ability to continue being appreciative. So we included it in the Array, with the intention of later exploring with Kendall whether or not this was her experience, as well.

The complete initial Belief Template, then, looks like this:

Initial Belief Template

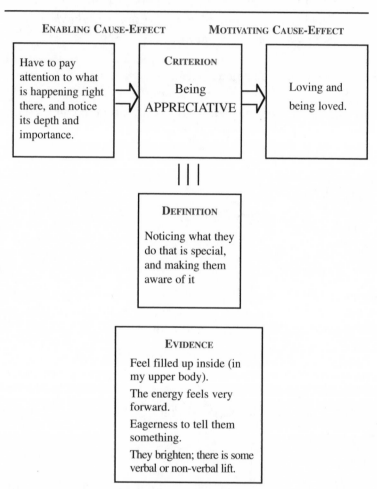

ENABLING CAUSE-EFFECT   MOTIVATING CAUSE-EFFECT

Have to pay attention to what is happening right there, and notice its depth and importance.

CRITERION

Being APPRECIATIVE

Loving and being loved.

DEFINITION

Noticing what they do that is special, and making them aware of it

EVIDENCE

Feel filled up inside (in my upper body).

The energy feels very forward.

Eagerness to tell them something.

They brighten; there is some verbal or non-verbal lift.

SUPPORTING BELIEF

It's there; I just need to keep searching.

STRATEGIES

PRIMARY STRATEGY

The unusual complexity of Kendall's Primary Strategy was reduced considerably by dividing it into three *sub-strategies*: Keep Attentive, Enjoy the Details, and Look for Deeper Meaning. These sub-strategies are operating more or less simultaneously when she is being passionate about something.

You will notice that we do not include in the Array many of the strategy pieces Kendall reveals, some of which we even wrote down during the elicitation. For instance, when she is working with her clients on the telephone, "...I picture them right there with me [gesturing], right in front of me." As useful as this strategy may be, it is relevant to her ability to "work effectively with clients on the telephone," and not to the ability we were eliciting, which is being passionate *about* the work she does.

You will also notice that we express Strategy steps as instructions to follow, rather than leaving them in the "I do this" form that your exemplar is likely to use. Because a strategy is essentially a set of internal and external behaviors to follow, we have found that putting the Strategy in the form of direct instruction makes it easier for us to follow and use.

KEEP ATTENTIVE

"Sitting forward," was the first strategy element we noted in the elicitation. As we mentioned regarding Kendall's Evidence, the feeling of "forward energy" is essential to sitting forward and therefore important to add to this Strategy step as well. She also talked about the tension of readiness in her body:

> Kendall: But it's sitting forward—so I'm not leaning back—*and there's probably a certain amount of tension in my body of readiness.*"

This seemed to us to be a part of sitting forward; we could see that tension when she sat forward, and we found when we tried it that the tension of readiness was likewise connected for us to sitting forward. So we described this element of her Strategy as, **"Sit upright, with forward energy and the tension of 'readiness.'"**

"Seeing the Big Picture" is exactly what Kendall said when first referring to this step in her Strategy. But putting it this way did not clearly convey our impression that, for Kendall, the Big Picture is in some sense *always there* in her experience, ready to be accessed in relation to what she is noticing at the time:

> Kendall: ...it's like I'm seeing the big picture and at the same time seeing the details. So if I'm working with somebody, I'm seeing the big picture of where we're going...
>
> I'm constantly checking in, Are we making progress towards that big picture?...
>
> And then I'm checking in with the details to, you know, sorting for, okay, if what we're talking about right now, is it moving us toward this big picture?

In order to capture this sense of the Big Picture constantly hovering in the background when she is being passionate about something, we altered this step to read, **"Hold the Big Picture."** (We did not end up including her question, "Are we making progress towards that big picture?" in her Paying Attention strategy because we later recognized that this question more properly belongs in her strategy for Finding Deeper Meaning.)

"Asking questions inside or outside": As originally captured during the elicitation, this Strategy step suggests that any questions can be asked. But it is clear from the many examples she gives that Kendall is asking particular kinds of questions:

> Kendall: Because when I've fallen out of paying attention, I'm usually not asking myself questions; I'm usually telling myself about other stuff. Usually I'm worrying about something...
>
> So, to translate that to riding, when I'm riding I'm asking questions of my own body posture. Are my elbows at my sides? you know, whatever...It depends on what I'm working on. [...] Do I have my thumb enough on the reins? Are my arms still loose? [...] Then I also ask questions about my horse. Is he falling on his shoulder?

> Is he straight? Is he, you know, does he feel relaxed in
> his body?

She is asking questions that take her attention to the details of the context in which she is passionate. So we rewrote this Strategy step as, **"Ask yourself questions that draw out the details and nuances of what you are attending to."**

The elicitation note, "Need to be flexible in terms of the detail we are working on," reflected what Kendall is doing when working with her horse. But she is also flexible in relation to her clients and her relationship with her husband:

> Kendall: And when you're dealing with an animal—just like with
> a human being—I think you have to be flexible. Because
> I may want to work on a particular thing with my horse
> and he's not—that's not what's going to work for him
> that day. You know, I expect this much of a range [hands
> wide] and his range that day is this much [hands close].
> And that's—so I have to adjust. And the same thing
> happens with a client.

Also, from a number of her examples, it was clear that being flexible was not only about what is being *worked on*, in the sense of having a specified goal. So we covered the more general sense of this with, **"Be flexible in terms of what to pursue."**

Initial Primary Strategy

PAY ATTENTION
- Sit upright, with forward energy and the tension of readiness.
- Hold the Big Picture.
- Ask yourself questions that draw out the details and nuances of what you are attending to.
- Be flexible in terms of what to pursue.

ENJOY DETAILS

One of the most striking aspects of Kendall's Strategy is that she enjoys the *details* of what she is passionate about. ("Somewhere in there, too, is, you know, this thing of noticing the details. I notice what I'm enjoying. I notice the details of what I'm enjoying.") For example:

Kendall: I'm noticing. With the feel of the air when it's crisp—I love riding when it's crisp, and the way it feels on my face. [...] ...the feel of the leather. The smells. There's a lot, particularly with horses there's a lot with smell.

I was just rubbing [Jaggy's] face, and he, you know, he just kind of turns and gives me what I call a 'horse hug'. And...just appreciating his body. And the smell. I love the smell of horses. That dirt and animal horse smell. Just appreciating that he's there, period. That he's there, that he's nice...he's a lovely horse. He's got a lot of personality. There's all kinds of things.

Also, it is clear that she actively looks for details to enjoy. Again, some examples:

Kendall: I'm looking for evidence to reinforce what I enjoy. So even when I used to do a lot of horse shows, which I don't anymore, but when I did them they were very exhausting. And I would be dead tired on my feet and dirty and grimy and sweaty from a very long day at the horse show. And I'd think...I would just notice, and relish, the sensation of being dirty and grimy and sweaty having spent time all day at this horse show. So even those types of things which are not necessarily pleasant, I somehow turn them into feeding my enjoyment. And that has to happen, otherwise I lose interest.

There is no real starting point for this feedback-feedforward relationship between noticing details and enjoying the context in which she is passionate. We decided to convey this tight loop like this:

Kendall described "cataloguing" what she enjoys in relation to her clients. But it was evident she does this in relation to her horseback riding and to her relationship with her husband, as well. So we expressed this Strategy step more generally as, **"Catalogue and store what you are appreciating so it more easily comes to your attention in the future."**

Initial Primary Strategy

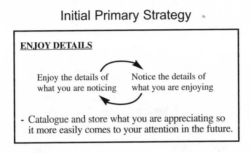

LOOK FOR DEEPER MEANING

Kendall is not only searching for details that she can enjoy, she is also searching for details that are *meaningful*. ("I'm searching for what is meaningful, I'm searching for clues.") From the many examples she gave it was evident that anything new or different is something possibly meaningful and worth examining. For instance:

Kendall: …a client will come to the call and they'll start in by saying, 'Okay, today I want to work on blah, blah, blah, blah, blah and, by the way, I got a couple of new clients last week, but what I really want to work on is this over here.' And I'll say, 'Okay, wait a second. Did I just hear you say you got two new clients last week?' And they'll say, 'Yes.' And I'll tell them, 'Let's just stop for a moment,' and 'I have questions about that.'

So we put down **"Notice anything different or new"** as the first step in this part of her Strategy.

We took the next step just as she described it. That is, to recognize that **"Anything that is a forward movement (a step in alignment with where you/they want to go), or a stretch (able to do something you/they were not able to do before), is meaningful."**

For us, the third step seemed to be to ask questions that "deepen the meaning." The two questions that she typically asks are, "How is this important?" and "What does this mean?" Answering these questions is in relation to the Big Picture.

"Deepen the meaning" suggests that the meaning is already established. However when we tried on her Strategy, it became clear that what is actually happening at this point is that the meaning is being revealed or discovered *through* these questions. A "forward movement" signals that there is something meaningful "here," and the questions establish what that meaning is. Nevertheless, because the initial Array is supposed to be in a form that the *exemplar* will recognize and resonate with as true for her, we kept her description of this strategy step: **"*Deepen* that meaning by discovering, 'How is this important?' and 'What does it mean?' in relation to 'the big picture.'"**

Initial Primary Strategy

<u>**LOOK FOR DEEPER MEANING**</u>

Search details and nuances for clues to what is meaningful.
- Notice anything that is different or new.
- Anything that is a forward movement (a step in alignment with where you/they want to go), or a stretch (able to do something you/they were not able to do before), is meaningful.
- Deepen that meaning by discovering...
    "How is this important?"
    "What does it mean?"
...in relation to the Big Picture.

SECONDARY STRATEGIES

As we noted earlier, Kendall's Secondary Strategies are in relation to her being able to "Pay Attention." When we asked her if it ever happens that she has difficulty in Look for Deeper Meaning, she answered:

> Kendall: I would have to guess that it does, but if it does happen it doesn't bother me. I mean, it's this . . . Maybe it doesn't happen. Maybe I am always finding it, because I'm really looking for evidence to support how much I enjoy this.

Because there are always details that she can put her attention on, any difficulties she might have are likely to be with respect to keeping her attention on those details.

When you are not as attentive as you would like to be:

We set down this Secondary Strategy just as Kendall described it:

1. **Notice that you've missed something.**

2. **Check posture (forward energy).**

3. **Go back to asking questions (either in your mind or verbally).**

When you are not at all attentive:

Recall that after asking Kendall about what she does when she is "not at all attentive," we asked her what she does when she "*cannot* be attentive":

> Kendall: Yeah, well that's this [pointing to her Strategy for "not at all attentive"]—what we just talked about. And I just think, You know what, I can't pay attention, so I'm just going to turn it over to them.

Because there is no real distinction for her between these two situations, we did not need to include a Secondary Strategy for "cannot be attentive."

In describing this Secondary Strategy we included her qualification that being "really tired" can lead to being not at all attentive. We thought this was important because it frames not being attentive as a natural result of being tired, rather than it leading her to question her passion for what she is doing. So the initial form of this Secondary Strategy is, **"(This may happen when you are really tired.) Ask an open-ended question, such as, 'What can I do that would be of most help to you right now?'"**

Initial Secondary Strategies

When you are not as attentive as you would like to be:
1. Notice that you've missed something.
2. Check posture (forward energy) and breathing.
3. Go back to asking questions (either in your mind or verbally).

When you are not at all attentive:
(This may happen when you are really tired.) Ask an open-ended question, such as "What can I do that would be of most help to you right now?"

EMOTIONS

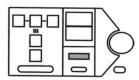

SUSTAINING EMOTION

The initial Array captures her Sustaining Emotion just as she described it, as a combination of "excited" and "grateful" that potentiate one another. We included her additional description of "grateful" in parenthesis because it helped us take on the particular way in which she experiences feeling grateful.

Sustaining Emotion

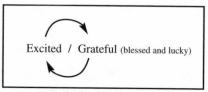

Excited / Grateful (blessed and lucky)

EXTERNAL BEHAVIOR

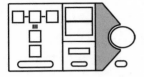

Again, Kendall's description of her External Behavior was clear and accessible to us, so we had only to set it down in the Array.

Initial External Behavior

> Body held upright, and leaning forward.
>
> I actually do the activities; I put my thoughts into action.
>
> Tell people what I am appreciating.

CONTRIBUTING FACTORS

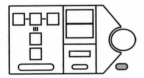

At the time of the elicitation, Kendall's "I'm not willing to live without passion in my life" struck us right away as a Contributing Factor (that is, it is not necessary for being passionate about something, but helpful). In reviewing the elicitation it also occurred to us that her remark, "I *know* what I enjoy," was also worth capturing as a Contributing Factor. When we included it in our own experience we found that it helped us be more deliberate in seeking out that which we enjoy.

Initial Contributing Factors

> I *know* what I enjoy.
>
> I'm not willing to live without passion in my life.

✻   ✻   ✻

Your initial Array may well be sufficiently detailed to be useful. That is, it captures enough of the patterns, and in enough detail, for you to begin to reproduce your exemplar's Ability.

Sometimes the process of organizing the information into an initial Array will reveal that there are aspects of the exemplar's Ability that you need to understand in greater depth. (It is for this reason that we suggested that, at the end of your elicitation, you arrange a short follow-up interview with your exemplar.) This was certainly the case for us with Kendall. In the next chapter we will go through the process of working with her to review and refine her Array. Before you read that chapter, we suggest that you take a few minutes to watch Segment 2 of the DVD, in which we work with her to refine the initial Array we created from the elicitation.

13

Completing the Array

As we noted in the beginning of the previous chapter, once the dust of the elicitation has settled, you are alone with your information. No longer involved in the back-and-forth of the elicitation itself, you are free to try on the exemplar's patterns yourself and to take the time to organize them into an initial Array. The reason it is an *initial* Array is that you will probably discover what we often discover: We need more information to make the Array into a workable model.

When we speak of Completing the Array, we are talking about making sure that the Array we end up with is one that is as comprehensive as it needs to be in order to *work* as a model for the ability. This is a *stage* that you will go through with your model. You may get through this stage in one brief follow-up with your exemplar, or it may take a series of meetings before you have what you need. Regardless of the number of evolutions your model must go through, the goal of this stage is to end up with an Array that both:

> **Resonates** (Matches your exemplar's experience)
> and
> **Works** (Gives you access to your exemplar's patterns)

At this stage we want to fill in any significant holes in the model. We do this by going back to the exemplar to do two things: (1) **Review,** to give the exemplar an opportunity to fill in holes she finds in our initial Array; and (2) **Clarify,** to give us an opportunity to have the exemplar help us fill in those holes we have found in the initial Array.

REVIEWING THE INITIAL ARRAY

Some of the ways in which you have described the patterns of experience in the initial Array may not, in fact, match your exemplar's experience of those patterns. Reviewing the Array with your exemplar is an opportunity for her to help you make important additions and refinements to the model.

Even though the Array describes your exemplar's experience, it is usually not effective to simply hand it to her and say "Well, what do you think?" What appears to you as meaningful snippets of description in a familiar format (the Array) is likely to appear to her as *disjointed* snippets of description in an arcane diagram. Instead, you create the environment for review by walking your exemplar through the initial Array. This means moving from one element of the Array to the next, describing and elaborating on them, *linking* them to other elements of the Array, and relating them to the context of the Ability. As an example, here is an excerpt from our walking Kendall through her review of the initial Array for "being passionate about something":

Graham: So, those are three contexts that you are passionate about.

Kendall: Yes.

Graham: And so in relation to your being passionate about them, what's important to you, *in* those contexts, is "being appreciative."

Kendall: Yes.

Graham: And that means, "noticing what they do that is special, and making them aware of it." [Kendall nods]…And the way you know that's happening is you "feel filled up inside [Kendall: Mmhm], in your upper body"…"the energy feels very forward" [Kendall: Mmhm]…"there's an eagerness to tell them something, and they brighten… there's some verbal or nonverbal *lift* to them" as you say something to them [Kendall nodding: Mmhm]. Now, what *enables* that, what makes that *possible* is "you're *paying* attention to what's happening right there [Kendall: Mmhm], and noticing its depth and importance."

Kendall: [nodding] I had an experience of that this morning when I was riding my horse…

This makes it much easier for your exemplar to relate the descriptive shorthand of the Array to her actual experience, which is precisely what you want her to be doing. You want this because, as you take your exemplar through the Array, she will be comparing your description with her own experience. The discrepancies will jump out at her and she will not let them pass. Instead, your exemplar will feel compelled to put you on the right path. This is, of course, just what you want and need. (You will see examples of Kendall correcting our initial Array in this way during the "Review and Clarify" segment of the DVD.)

As we did in the previous chapter, we will now use our review and clarification work with Kendall as a way of letting you in on the processes and thinking involved in this stage of completing the Array.

"Being Passionate About Something" — *Reviewing the Initial Array*

BELIEF TEMPLATE

All of the elements of the Belief Template seemed to resonate with Kendall just as we had captured them. In fact, it immediately moved her to relate an experience of it manifesting itself that same morning while riding her horse:

> Kendall: Yeah. Just getting on and thinking just how good it feels, and just the motion of walking along, and just noticing the motion and really relishing that, the nice breeze, the pretty scenery…and, yes, so I did have that feeling of being filled up. And I just sat taller, and I think *I* brightened. I don't know that I said anything to my horse at that moment! [laughs] But I did it by saying to myself, This is fantastic!

> Graham: Yeah, well, one of the things you said during the elicitation was that you use this for yourself, *on* yourself, too.

> Kendall: Right.

As it turned out, this was a helpful example because it alerted us to the fact that we had described both her Definition and a part of her Evidence as though they related *only* to other people: "Noticing what *they* do that is special"; "Eagerness to tell *them* something"; "*They* brighten." In fact, she herself can also be the subject of "being appreciative." That is, she can notice what she is doing that is special and make herself aware of it. Accordingly, we broadened the Definition of "Being Appreciative" to **"Noticing what is special, and**

making myself or others aware of it":

```
┌─────────────────────┐
│      CRITERION      │
│                     │
│       Being         │
│    APPRECIATIVE     │
│                     │
│                     │
└─────────────────────┘

        │ │ │

┌─────────────────────┐
│     DEFINITION      │
│                     │
│  Noticing what is   │
│  special, and       │
│  making myself or   │
│  others aware of it.│
└─────────────────────┘
```

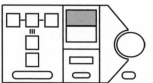 **PRIMARY STRATEGY – PAY ATTENTION**

In reviewing her Primary Strategy for Pay Attention, one thing that did not quite fit for Kendall was the description "sit upright" in the first element of the Strategy:

Kendall: I was thinking—it's a small example, but it matters—I was thinking how I could be sitting on the couch with my husband...for example, last week. And we were just quietly reading. We hadn't said a word in about two hours. And it was such an intense pleasure to be able to sit there and just be with each other and be reading and not have to be doing anything. And I remember noticing it and saying to him, "I just am *loving* this. I'm just loving sitting here with you like this." ***And I didn't exactly sit forward at that time.*** So that was the one nuance I wanted to bring out. But there was still a feeling of filling up in my upper body, definitely. ***It was a sense of coming forward. I don't know that anyone would*** *have seen me come forward.*

David: So it goes back to, you're talking about the *energy* feels
very forward.

Kendall: The energy feels very forward, yes.

David: That may translate into your body moving forward
or not—

Kendall: Right, right.

From this we realized that we would need to change this element to
emphasize the "sense of coming forward," and offer "sitting upright" as a
possible expression *of* having that sense.

Kendall had no comments or corrections to make to her Primary Strategy
for Enjoy Details. And when we reviewed Look for Deeper Meaning, she
confirmed that "I have to notice the details first, and *then* find the deeper
meaning, *connect* it to the deeper meaning," which matches the way we had
represented this relationship in the initial Array.

She then went on to explain that, despite the fact that she is always
looking for a deeper meaning:

Kendall: ...I don't feel like I'm attached to it *being*
there...although I would imagine if I didn't find it in any
parts of my life I might become *very* attached to *that*!
[laughs]...but, so it's not like...I don't feel like I try and
make meaning where there isn't one. Sometimes like,
You know what, oop! That has no meaning! Move on.
And that's fine. But I'm always asking that question
internally: Is there a deeper meaning here? Is there
something meaningful?

This seemed important to note because it takes finding deeper meaning out
of the compulsive realm of *must find* and puts it into the realm of possibility:
Is it there? (We will return to this point in the next section on Clarifying
the Array.)

THE REST OF THE INITIAL ARRAY

Kendall agreed with, and had nothing to add to, how we had described her Secondary Strategies, Sustaining Emotions, External Behavior, and Contributing Factors for her ability to be passionate about something.

CLARIFYING THE INITIAL ARRAY

It is likely that in the process of creating the initial Array you discovered holes in your understanding of the exemplar's patterns of experience and behavior. Typically, these holes make themselves known when you try on the patterns you have captured in the initial Array and find that one or another of them does not *work* (that is, does not seem to move you toward manifesting the Ability). Perhaps more detail is needed regarding the nature of a particular experience; perhaps more detail is needed regarding exactly how to do something; or perhaps something is missing altogether in the initial Array.

In any case, the answers to your questions will be found in your exemplar. Because of your growing familiarity with the patterns underlying the Ability, your follow-up questions of your exemplar are likely to be more pointed and your understanding of the answers deeper. Just as in the original elicitation, however, you are still at the stage of capturing your exemplar's experience as faithfully as possible and, so, you want to record your exemplar's experience just as she describes it. ˙

"Being Passionate About Something" — *Clarifying the Initial Array*

We had accomplished the first step of reviewing the initial Array with Kendall. Her responses had allowed us either to refine or confirm our initial Array. However, there were still some points we needed to clarify for ourselves. In particular, we had questions about her Primary and Secondary Strategies, her Sustaining Emotion, and a Supporting Belief.

PRIMARY STRATEGY – PAY ATTENTION

When we tried to "hold the Big Picture," we realized that we were not sure what *constituted* a Big Picture. We asked Kendall, "What *is* a Big Picture?":

Kendall: What do you mean, "What is a big picture?" [laughs]

Graham: So, what is *in* these big pictures? What do they represent?

Kendall: The big picture…*it's definitely a sense of being big, you know, [arcing her arms over her head] over me. Over and a little bit in front of.* When I think of big picture of a client, or my horse, or a relationship, that's where it is. …It's *not* crystal clear. It's actually, I mean I feel like at any moment in time I could fill in clearly a detail. That would not be an issue. But when I just think of a big picture, *it's definitely in color, and it's fuzzy.* Which, I've thought about this before—about how I do this— and I *like* keeping it fuzzy like that because it means that, *I* feel like it means that I have flexibility…because the big picture can change.

　　[…]

David: In relation to things that you are *passionate* about, is there any quality, anything that *has* to be a part *of* that picture?

Kendall: *Enjoyment has to be there.* I have to continue to…I *have* to be enjoying myself.

Graham: And you see that in the big picture somehow?

Kendall: I do, actually. I'm trying to think of how I see that…*I think the color has something to do with it, and the colors are very pleasing to me, to my eye.* It's interesting… I'll just contrast it by thinking of photography, which I'm mildly interested in as an adult. (I did a lot of it as a teenager.) And when I think of doing photography, it's *not* up there [hands held high, in front], it's not in color, it's down here [hands held low], it's black and white, it's small. So there's the difference! [laughs] It's not some rainbow.

Now we have a better idea of what constitute the perceptual qualities of a Big Picture, namely, that it is experienced as being bigger than oneself, it is held above and a bit in front of oneself, and it is an image that is in color and "fuzzy." "Enjoyment has to be there" is an important quality that needs to be a part of a Big Picture. To see if a specific example would reveal more, we asked her to describe her Big Picture in relation to her horse:

Kendall: The big picture is that…having a horse has always been a dream of mine. Having *this* horse, he's like my dream horse. He is. **He's the horse of a lifetime. And so that to me is the big picture, it's having this horse I've always dreamed of. So, it's like the ideal. Yeah, That's an interesting thing. It is like the ideal,** and I'm just trying that on with my clients…Because I do, I formulate a big picture. When someone is about to hire me, I'm immediately thinking of, Okay, what's the big picture here? And I think to translate that it would be, **What's ideal? Ideally, what would this be like?** What would their business be like? Because my job is to help them get towards that. So with my horse, it's what's the—**the big picture is keeping in mind this ideal** I have about having a horse. **It's the fantasy, actually!** [laughs] Same thing with the relationship, you know. **It's the fantasy!**

[…]

You know I said the word "fantasy" and laughed, but I don't think it's actually that far off base. It's…it's like, Wouldn't it be great if this happened! [inscribes a "big picture" in the air] I'm holding this image of, Wouldn't it be great!

Describing the Big Picture as something that is an "ideal, dream, or fantasy" made it *much* easier for us to relate to what a Big Picture is, and to generate one for ourselves. Kendall then helped us make a distinction between a goal and a Big Picture: a Big Picture is where you are headed, and the goals are the things you do to "progress towards the dream":

Kendall: And it's the same thing with the horse and being in a relationship. It's that dream and constantly doing things and evaluating things to…I was going to say, "To make progress towards the dream…" Yeah, *it is mostly making progress towards the dream. Sometimes* I actually stop and say, Wow, I'm *in* the dream! [laughs] And that's really special. *But I tend to think of it more as moving towards the dream. And I don't have to have progress in big leaps and bounds.* I'm not a patient person, but I'm *very* patient with that. That's enough to satisfy.

This supplied a piece we needed to make the connect between the details she is noticing and the Big Picture. That is, in the details she finds—and appreciates—the evidence of moving toward the ideal represented in the Big Picture. We added these details regarding the Big Picture to Kendall's Primary Strategy, as well as the correction she had made during the review of the initial Array (regarding having *forward energy*, rather than simply sitting forward):

Primary Strategy

> **KEEP ATTENTIVE**
> * Upright posture, with forward energy and the tension of *readiness*.
> * Be flexible in terms of what to pursue.
> * Ask questions that draw out the details and nuances of what you are attending to.
> * Ask whether the details you are noticing are taking you toward the Big Picture (a colorful but fuzzy image of the ideal, the dream, the fantasy).

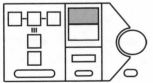

PRIMARY STRATEGY – LOOK FOR DEEPER MEANING

We realized that we had neglected to specify the difference between the two questions Kendall asks herself: "How is this important?" and "What does it mean?" We began by asking her "Do you ask both?"

Kendall: *Yeah, I think they both have to be there.* They get asked *sooo* rapidly. Yeah.

Graham: Are they *different* questions for you?

Kendall: Yes.

Graham: What's the difference?

Kendall: Yeah. So the first one of…

Graham: "How's this important?"

Kendall: "How's this important?"… ***"How is this important," it's a searching question to me. It's very much—it sends me searching…*** for, How is this important. And the second one of…

Graham: "What does this mean?"

Kendall: Yeah, "What does this mean?" It's funny, because it happens so fast that I'm not breaking them apart…It's almost like, "What does this mean?"…***It's like the first one sends me searching on possibilities, and the second one finds— grabs the possibility. If it's there. It may not be there, you know, and I move on. In other words, I don't make there be meaning if there isn't any meaning there.***

Now her Primary Strategy for looking for deeper meaning was opening up to us. The distinction she made between the two questions told us how to use them in our own experience: Ask "How is this important?" to initiate searching for possible meanings; then ask "What does it mean?" to select a *deeper meaning* from those possibilities. However, we still wanted to know just how a possible meaning gets identified as meaningful:

Kendall: Yeah, "What does this mean?" ***It's that deeper feeling.*** It's so interesting how the deeper feeling is so different than the big picture. I mean, really, ***the deeper meaning is like, woomf!*** [dropping her hands and body, laughs] ***And it's heavy and it's dark and it's murky and it's, like, here.*** [hands cupped low] ***It's in the gut.*** And the big picture is up here. [inscribing an arc over her head]

Graham: So, you say they're different.

Kendall: Very.

Graham: We talked about what's in the big picture—

Kendall: It actually, then it goes, it relates to the big picture.

Graham: How?

Kendall: I mean, I'm looking to see, What does this mean?—you know, I'm looking for the deeper meaning—and then it's like I check in: How does that fit with the bigger picture? *Because if it doesn't fit, then I find that interesting, and then I think, Well, does the big picture need to shift, or...? Maybe, maybe not; I don't know. To me, the deeper meaning doesn't shift. If it's there, it's there.*

We already knew from the elicitation that she relates the deeper meaning to the Big Picture, but this additional description made it clear *what* she is checking for, which is, "Does it *fit* with the bigger picture?" In addition, we learned that if something is meaningful but does not fit with the Big Picture she will consider whether or not some change needs to be made in that Big Picture (since deeper meanings are more fundamental and do not shift, while Big Pictures are "dreams" or "fantasies").

We still wanted to better understand how to *grab* the deeper meaning, so we asked her to describe an example so that we could explore it more closely with her:

Kendall: It's very difficult to put words to it, to how *important* being around horses and riding is.

David: So, that awareness of how important that—*knowing* that—

Kendall: Yes.

David: ...is that one of those "low" experiences you were talking about—

Kendall: Yes. It's like this Oomph!

David: Oomph! Actually, you know when I try it, the words that go off in my head with that Oomph is, "That's *true.*"

Kendall: Yeah. Absolutely.

David: That's *so.* That's just *true.*

Kendall: It's like, it's immutable.

David: Right, it's immutable. And then you somehow connect that to, or relate that to this bigger picture that you are having—

Kendall: Yeah, and it's interesting. I was just thinking about it yesterday, how I know I am not—as a human being, I am *not* the fact that I ride, or I am not the fact that I do coaching, or whatever. And the dichotomy there is that at the same time it *is* who I am. I mean, it's how I define myself from the inside. (Makes it a little scary if I ever couldn't ride! That's the only…well, yeah, actually it's been very chaotic during those times.) So it's like, because it's like, **This is an expression of who I am,** *actually is what it is. This an expression of who I am. Just like my clothes are an expression of who I am. So they really matter to me…* And then the big picture is that fantasy! That's how it reads; it's like, *This* really matters [gesturing low] and *here's* this fantasy [gesturing high]. And when the two go hand and glove, life is fabulous.

David: Yeah, when you're either *there* [pointing up] or *moving* towards there.

Kendall: Yeah!

Kendall has given us a description of when she finds deeper meaning: Any detail or nuance that is an expression of who she is (as in this case, or who someone else is in other cases), is meaningful. Another way to say that is, Meaningful details will be those that are expressions of what is true for (about) you. The refinements we needed to add to this part of the Primary Strategy, then, were (1) the difference between the two questions she asks herself, (2) relating new things she notices to who she is as a person (or others are) as a way of determining if it is a meaningful detail, and (3) considering whether a new and meaningful detail necessitates a change in her Big Picture:

Primary Strategy

LOOK FOR DEEPER MEANING

1. Notice anything that is different or new.
2. "How is this important?" (*Is* this meaningful?)
   i.e. Is it a stretch (able to do something you/they were not able to do before), forward movement (a step in alignment with where you/they want to go), backward movement. etc.?
3. "What does it mean in terms of who I (they/we) *really* am?"
4. How does that relate to the Big Picture? (Does it necessitate changing the Big Picture?)
5. Celebrate and enjoy this development.

SECONDARY STRATEGY – LOOK FOR DEEPER MEANING

When we were creating the initial Array it seemed that the important Secondary Strategies would all be in relation to Pay Attention, because so much of Kendall being passionate hinges on her *noticing* details. Once we had a clearer idea of how she goes about looking for Deeper Meaning, however, we recognized that finding the connection between what she is noticing and its being an expression of who she (or someone else) is may not always be obvious. We asked her, What do you do when you suspect there is a deeper meaning, but you are having difficulty in identifying what that meaning is?:

Kendall: *Well, the first thing I do is just question, Is there a deeper meaning or not? There isn't in everything, you know. Sometimes a cigar is just a cigar. And it's truly a felt sense. If there is a felt sense that there is a deeper meaning, then I pursue it.* And…you want to know how I pursue it?… *I'll ask a question.* I think a lot in terms of questions, like I said before. And generally I will ask the question out loud to the person I'm working with. Yeah. You know, *it's always a "what" question.* Always. "What" questions are my favorites. And it might be *something along the line of, "What's really important to you about this?"*

    […]

Graham: How far do you go in pursuing a deeper meaning?

Kendall: I'm not relentless. If I'm working with another person, I'm not relentless, because that would be rude… or just insensitive, I think.

David: And with yourself?

Kendall: With myself I'll pursue it.

Graham: You're insensitive to yourself? [laughing]

Kendall: I can be *very* insensitive to myself! [laughing] So I work a million hours and *drive* myself. Yeah. Actually, though, with myself I have a luxury, because *I'm willing to ask myself the question, and if I don't come up with an*

> *answer I really trust that the answer is there.* I'm very
> aware that I do this. I trust that it's there and that it will
> come. And so—you know I take it back; I'm *not*
> relentless with myself [pursuing a deeper meaning],
> because I know that will just drive it away. But *if I ask
> the question and tell myself, "This is important. I want
> to know," I can let it go and it will come to me.* Yeah, and
> I trust that. And it always happens.

If the deeper meaning is not obvious, the first thing she does is ask herself if there *is* a deeper meaning to be found in this instance. She does not assume that everything is fraught with deep meaning, but instead trusts her feelings to indicate whether or not something has a deeper meaning. If there *does* seem to be deeper meaning, she pursues it by asking herself (or, if it is about someone else, them) a question like, "What's really important to me (you) about this?" If she gets an answer, fine; if not, she does not try to wring one out. Instead, she flags it as important by telling herself, "This is important. I want to know," and then lets go of trying to figure it out, trusting that "it will come to me." So we added to the Secondary Strategies:

Secondary Strategy

WHEN THE DEEPER MEANNNG IS NOT OBVIOUS:

1. Ask yourself if there *is* a deeper meaning, trusting your feelings to tell you whether or not there is.
   - If not, drop it. ("Sometimes a cigar is just a cigar.")
2. If there *does* seem to be a deeper meaning, ask yourself "What's really important to me/them/us about this?"
3. If you do not get an answer, tell yourself "This is important; I want to know," and trust that the answer will eventually come to you.

SUSTAINING EMOTION

It was clear to us how feeling "excited" would enhance (feed) feeling "grateful," but we were not sure how the other side of the loop worked. We asked Kendall, How does feeling "grateful" feed feeling "excited"?:

> Kendall: I really love appreciating being grateful. I know it sounds kind of funny, but *I appreciate being grateful. I appreciate the fact that I can be grateful. That I'm that aware of what I have, and that I just feel very lucky and I really enjoy feeling lucky. And so I find it really exciting to be appreciating the fact that I'm grateful.* [laughs]
>
> [...]
>
> And I appreciate a *lot* of different things. I appreciate, you know, wearing beautiful clothes, and I appreciate the flowers...I appreciate all *kinds* of things. And I get excited that I notice those things. I get excited that I'm paying attention. Because paying attention is important to me. So maybe that's where the closure of the loop is: Paying attention is important. *Really* important. So I get excited that I'm paying attention.

Kendall's explanation did not change how we represented her Sustaining Emotion in the Array. It was very useful, however, as it helped us get the "excited/grateful" loop whirling in our own experience.

SUPPORTING BELIEF

As we worked on creating the initial Array, we were struck by Kendall explaining at one point, "If you are looking for something you tend to find it," and at another point the similar, "It's there; I just need to keep searching." She expressed these as basic truths and with an intensity that typically indicates a Supporting Belief. What is more, when we stepped into being passionate about something with this belief added in, it significantly affected our ability to *be* passionate. We wanted to check this out with Kendall:

> Graham: ...We had the sense that this particular belief—that "It's there, and you just need to keep searching"—went through other things, too, like finding details and

nuances which are meaningful—

Kendall: Absolutely. And actually, even though, you know, sometimes I have to do tasks that I don't particularly enjoy—you know, any type of routine production work I don't really enjoy, and I tend to make mistakes at it—but if I have to do it for a short period of time, I'm looking to say, Okay, what is it about this that I can enjoy? Again, because I'm not—and I know this is a little different than what you are talking about, but I think it applies—because I'm not willing to sit there and do something I completely don't enjoy. That's just no fun, and life's too short. I love feeling in love with what I'm doing. And so even in the situation, in the context of not doing something I particularly enjoy, I'm looking for some element, some little nuance, either in the detail of what I'm doing or how it relates to a bigger over-arching theme in my life. Yeah, I believe there's *so* much to be passionate about. The only trouble is having enough time. The trouble isn't in finding it, the trouble is in having enough time.

Graham: So it's always based on the fact that it's *there*.

Kendall: It's there!

Clearly, believing that "It's there; I just need to keep searching" is significant since it supports an essential aspect of Kendall's being passionate about something, namely the ability to discover details that she can attend to and appreciate. So we included it as a Supporting Belief:

Supporting Belief

"It's there; I just need to keep searching."

On pages 154 and 155, then, is the final Array for Kendall's ability to be passionate about something...

THE FINAL ARRAY FOR KENDALL

ENABLING CAUSE-EFFECT   MOTIVATING CAUSE-EFFECT

| Have to pay attention to what is happening right there, and notice its depth and importance. | ⇒ | CRITERION

Being APPRECIATIVE | ⇒ | Loving and being loved. |

| | |

DEFINITION

Noticing what is special, and making myself or others aware of it"

EVIDENCE

Feel filled up inside (in my upper body).

The energy feels very forward.

Eagerness to tell them something.

They brighten; there is some verbal or non-verbal lift.

SUPPORTING BELIEF

It's there; I just need to keep searching.

PRIMARY STRATEGY

PAY ATTENTION

* Upright posture, with forward energy and the tension of readiness.
* Be flexible in terms of what to pursue.
* Ask questions that draw out the details and nuances of what you are attending to.
* Ask whether the details you are noticing are taking you toward the Big Picture (a colorful but fuzzy image of the ideal, the dream, the fantasy).

ENJOY DETAILS

* Enjoy the details of   Notice the details of
  what you are noticing   what you are enjoying

* Recognize how what you are enjoying connects you to the Big Picture.
* Turn unpleasant things into something that can feed your enjoyment.
* Catalogue and store what you are appreciating so it more easily comes to your attention in the future. ("I know what I enjoy.")

LOOK FOR DEEPER MEANING

1. Notice anything that is different or new.
2. "How is this important?" (Is this meaningful?)
   i.e. Is it a stretch (something you/they were not able to do before), forward movement (in alignment with where you/they want to go), backward movement, etc.?
3. "What does it mean in terms of who I (they/we) really am?"
4. How does that relate to the Big Picture? (Does it necessitate changing the Big Picture?)
5. Celebrate and enjoy this development.

SECONDARY STRATEGIES

When you are not as Attentive as you would like to be:
1. Notice that you've missed something.
2. Check posture (forward energy) and breathing.
3. Go back to asking questions (either in your mind or verbally).

When you are not at all Attentive:
   If you are really tired, you may have to give up trying to be attentive. If you can't come back to being attentive (usually by asking questions), let it go.

When the Deeper Meaning is not obvious:
1. Ask yourself if there *is* a deeper meaning, trusting your feelings to tell you whether or not there is. (If not, drop it. "Sometimes a cigar is just a cigar")
2. If there *does* seem to be a deeper meaning, ask yourself, "What's really important to me/them/us about this?"
3. If you do not get an answer, tell yourself, "This is important; I want to know," and trust that the answer will eventually come to you.

SUSTAINING EMOTION

Excited / Grateful (feeling Blessed and Lucky)

EXTERNAL BEHAVIOR

Body held upright.

.

ABILITY

BEING PASSIONATE ABOUT SOMETHING

Caring so deeply about something that you engage in it eagerly and often, and in many different ways.

I actually do the activities; I put my thoughts into action.

Tell people what I am appreciating.

CONTRIBUTING FACTORS

I'm not willing to live without passion in my life.

14

Acquisition

The description of how a wing provides lift is not itself a wing. If a wing is to become something that carries us upward, we must turn the description of how a wing works into something tangible, something that has a presence in the world. Similarly, a model is not the Ability that it is a model of; to manifest the Ability, we must embody the structure described in the model. The structure you have elicited and refined into a model needs to become a part of you, transforming from information on a page into experience and behavior.

Because of the stepping-in you did during elicitation, some of this transition has undoubtedly already occurred. When you were stepping in you were not only testing the patterns of experience your exemplar described, but often learning them as well. Still, though you have *tasted* all of the elements of the model, they are probably not yet digested, that is, not yet operating systemically and systematically, smoothly and automatically in your experience. The model still needs to be *acquired*.

In general, acquiring an Ability involves first ACCESSING the elements of the model into your experience, then INTEGRATING them. Before going into detail about these two stages of acquisition, however, we need to first introduce you to what you will be accessing and integrating, namely, *reference experiences*.

Reference Experiences

Our lives are filled with experiences that we try to make sense of and learn from. In the process of doing this each of us puts together a subjective world that is expressed (put into action) through our behavior. This is not necessarily something we do consciously or intentionally. Making sense of experience is something that our bodies and minds naturally do as a way of learning to respond appropriately to the world. As you make more and more sense (meaning, connections, significance), a map for living emerges. This is a personal map, an integration of your experiences into a map of the world.

Experiences that create these personal maps we call reference experiences.

Reference experiences are any experiences that form our maps of the world. Our reference experiences establish everything from our simplest instrumental behaviors to our loftiest abstractions and philosophies, from not touching a hot stove to touching the mysteries of life. For example:

> Lee Atwater (the U.S. Republican National Committee Chairman in the late 1980's) was aggressively partisan and notorious for his ruthless politicking (the nadir of which was the negative presidential campaign he ran on behalf of George Bush in 1988). In 1991, at the age of 39, Atwater discovered he had a benign brain tumor. "It's going to be hard for me to be as tough on people," he said. "Forget money and power. I had no idea how wonderful people are...What a way to have to find out."

> Prince Sultan ibn Salman al Saud of Saudi Arabia, the first Arab astronaut, described his experience aboard the space shuttle Discovery, an experience that palpably brought home to him the need for world peace: "On the first and second day of the flight, we were all noticing our countries, saying, 'That's my home.' By the third day, you only see continents. By the fifth day, you see only the Earth—it becomes one place, your home...It's an amazing feeling."[1]

A stroll through your personal history will provide you with your own examples of reference experiences that changed your world. These experiences may have been pleasant or unpleasant, they may have lasted only a moment or spanned days, weeks, or months. But in every case the effect was the same: the experience was sufficiently compelling to redraw in some subtle or profound way the map of your world.

Once new features are written onto our personal maps, those features tend to preserve themselves. They do this first by acting as experiential guides that focus your attention on whatever fits with them. For instance, if you come to believe that people are wonderful, you will look for, be sensitive to, and notice instances of people being wonderful. Having your attention on examples of people being wonderful naturally affects the judgments you make about them, your responses to them, your behavior toward them, and so on. (As Lee Atwater

---

[1] "Lee Atwater": Tribune News Service, March 1991. "Prince Sultan ibn Salman al Saud": Los Angeles Times, September 15, 1985.

acknowledged, "It's going to be hard for me to be as tough on people.")

Our maps also tend to preserve themselves by acting as filters on our experience, providing the basis for deleting or explaining away anything that contradicts them. A common example of this is found in how we typically respond to politicians. If a politician we think is "bad" does something "good," we are likely to explain it away as a venal attempt to advance some hidden agenda, and so on. When a politician we consider "good" does something "bad," however, we are just as likely to excuse it with explanations such as, "He was forced to do it" or "It was a mistake anyone could have made."

This focusing and filtering of experience by your map reinforces the map *as it is*. As you live through your map, it naturally gets stronger by confirming itself again and again. Our reference experiences are very important, then, because they establish the self-reinforcing personal maps that become the world of our experience and behavior.

We have been talking about reference experiences as though it only takes one to establish a new feature in your map of the world. That can be true, provided that the one experience is of sufficient *magnitude* (strength or power) to establish a change in your map. For example, undoubtedly Lee Atwater had met many wonderful people in his life, but none of those experiences were of sufficient magnitude to instill in him the idea that "people are wonderful." That epiphany had to wait until he had the intense experience of interacting with people as they helped him deal with his brain tumor. Each of us has many examples of these map-changing moments in our personal histories. They are obvious in some of the big events of our lives. You will also find them in many of the tiny, often momentary events (like the morning you spotted a homeless man doing the New York Times crossword, and realized that one does not need to be ignorant to be homeless).

Having an experience of sufficient magnitude is not the only way our maps of the world change. They can also be changed through the *repetition* of experiences. That is, having a certain kind of experience again and again can eventually create a set of references capable of bringing about a change in the terrain of your subjective world. For example, one instance of working hard at something and succeeding may not itself have been a compelling enough experience to convince you that, "If I work hard, I will succeed." But a series of experiences of hard work leading to success may *stack* themselves until their combined weight topples you into believing that "Hard work leads to success."

In terms of acquiring an Ability you have modeled, the significance of reference experiences is that they are the means through which you will access that model into your experience. A new Ability is not stuck onto who you are, like a note glued to a map; it is integrated into the map. As our brief review of reference experiences makes clear, the way something gets integrated into our personal maps is through having experiences that make that perception, idea, or behavior real and tangible to us. What transfers the model from the page into experience are reference experiences.[2]

Access: Establishing the Model in your Experience

The first step in acquiring the Ability that you have modeled is to make sure that you can easily access the elements of that Ability into your experience. As we said, you have already gained access to at least some of the elements of the Ability in the process of eliciting the Array. Now you need to make sure that you have ready access to the whole Array.

The process for gaining ready access is essentially the same for all of the elements:

a. For each element of the Array, find your own reference experiences that allow you to access that element into your experience, then...

b. In imagination, rehearse using that element in the context in which you want to manifest the Ability.

We talk about finding your own reference experiences as though they are already there, just waiting to be retrieved. And for the most part, they are. There is an ocean of experience in each of us ready and waiting to be fished. In fact, experiences that can serve as references for the patterns described in any model are almost certainly already somewhere in your personal history— in your ocean of experience—waiting to be retrieved and put to use. The untapped richness of your personal history makes it possible to confidently assume that you already have the experiences you need, and that you have only to bring them to the surface of your experience. (We will talk about what to do if you are having difficulty in accessing reference experiences—as well as other acquisition difficulties—later in this chapter.)

During acquisition these previously free floating experiences are being gathered in support of your acquiring a particular Ability. This gives those

---

[2] More detail on reference experiences can be found in a paper by Gordon, "Reference Experiences: Guardians of Coherence and Instigators of Change," in Zeig and Gilligan, *Brief Therapy: Myths, Methods, and Metaphors*. Also, for those interested in exploring the relationship between reference experiences and change, there is no better resource than the therapeutic case work of Milton H. Erickson. In particular, Jay Haley's book on Erickson's work, *Uncommon Therapy*, is a gold mine of examples.

experiences a relevance and significance they did not have before. As we discussed above (in talking about the effects of reference experiences), once you have found a reference experience for an element, that element becomes experientially accessible to you. Because that element is now present in your experience, it naturally focuses and filters your attention in ways that fit with itself. The result is a growing snowball of reinforcing experiences for that element, which soon cements it into place.

Rehearsal

A young man was wandering around New York City, obviously lost. He stopped an old man who was passing by and asked, "How do I get to Carnegie Hall?" Noticing that the young man was carrying a violin case, the old man answered, "Practice, practice," and walked on. This is an old joke, but one worth remembering. You can have a wonderful instrument and sheets of beautiful music, but they don't play themselves; you have to practice playing them. We are in the same situation regarding model acquisition.

Ultimately, you will use the Ability you have modeled in real world situations. But before stepping out into those deeper waters, it is useful to rehearse that Ability in the safer pool of your imagination. Each time you rehearse manifesting the Ability you will increase your facility at accessing its structure. At the same time, you are strengthening the connection between being in the context and the accessing of that structure; that is, you are establishing the habit of manifesting the Ability when you need it.

In addition, rehearsing the Ability is an opportunity to get out the bugs. Even rehearsing in imagination can reveal potential difficulties. You may discover that an element you thought you had easy access to is really not yet in your experience. Or that some element of the structure bumps up against one of your beliefs or values, and needs to be addressed. Or that you are missing some important piece of information or structure that you need in order to make it all work for you. It is better to find and deal with as many of these stumbling blocks as you can during rehearsal rather than in the real world, where they might undermine your confidence, or even lead you to abandon your efforts to acquire the Ability.

THE ACQUISITION PROTOCOL

In the same way that no organ of your body is more important than another, no element of experience is more important than another. An Ability does not reside in any one element of experience, but in the collective acting and interacting of them all. Still, if we were building a home we would pour the foundation before erecting the walls, and we would put up walls before trying to put on a roof. The following sequence is one we have found naturally supports the acquisition of an Ability that has been modeled as an Array. This is essentially the same sequence we use in the DVD example of helping Kathy acquire Kendall's ability to be passionate about something:

Acquisition Protocol

1. Assess the ecology of having the Ability.

2. Connect having the Ability to satisfying one of your Prime Motivators.

3. Identify a PAST SITUATION in which you *really needed* the Ability.

4. Access the Criterion/Definition/Evidence and the Sustaining Emotion, then step into the PAST SITUATION while holding those elements in your experience. Practice this until you can access them easily.

   * Recognize how in satisfying the Criterion you are also satisfying your Prime Motivator.

5. Access reference experiences for any Supporting Beliefs, and take them into the PAST SITUATION.

6. Run through the Primary Strategy and External Behaviors in the PAST SITUATION, and practice them until they are working for you.

7. Recognize that the Enabling Cause-Effect is *true*.

8. Practice the entire Ability in *other* past situations, until you are sure that you can easily access the elements.

9. Think of *any* real-world difficulties that could arise (difficulties that could stop you from manifesting the Ability), and practice overcoming them by using Secondary Strategies.

10. Identify the next time you will need the Ability, and

rehearse manifesting it in that situation.

Let's take each of these steps one at a time and describe what they involve:

1. Assess the ecology of having the Ability.

Everyone understands that natural systems such as forests, deserts, and oceans establish their own ecologies; they establish systems of actions and corrections that maintain a particular balance. And we also recognize that introducing something new into any of those systems may dramatically shift their balance.

Like a forest or an ocean, each of us is also a natural system, and each of us has our own ecology. You have many examples of this in your life, such as when you moved from living alone to living with a mate, or changed jobs, or changed your work schedule. Behaviors, attitudes and abilities are also aspects of your ecology, and changing them can lead to establishing a new point of balance in your personal ecology. For instance, if you are someone who has in the past placed the needs of others first, then learning to be considerate of your own needs will necessarily change the choices you make, how you respond to others, and how they respond to you. Kendall talked about this during our review of her ability to be passionate:

Kendall: [The commitment of time and energy] is why I'm not passionate about photography. Because it's not as important as these other things.

David: As your body and your head knows, if you *did* become passionate about photography—

Kendall: It would take over.

David: It would take over other things, it would start crowding other things.

Kendall: Right.

David: Your dance card is pretty full.

Kendall: I was going to say, "I'm full up!" [laughs] And truthfully, the horse has been the constant. I *did* go seventeen years without having a horse, and finally decided that I was not willing to live without them anymore and got them back in my life [snaps her fingers] like that. Just appeared. But you're right about it taking over, and being a priority.

> And sometimes making tough decisions. You know,
> certainly my passion for my horse contributed to the
> demise of two marriages. It wasn't the *sole* contributor,
> but it was a factor. Certainly caused a lot of arguments.
> Because of the passion. And because a lot of other people,
> they're not willing…it's like, they're jealous of that. Just
> jealous of it. [shrugs] Sorry. [laughs] It's the way it is.

Before you began modeling the Ability you want to acquire, you probably thought only of what having it will do for you. Now that you *have* modeled it, you understand more specifically what having it will actually mean in terms of changes in thinking and behavior. This gives you a much better basis for considering how it will affect your life. The importance of this step is illustrated in the DVD example of acquisition with Kathy. When David raises the fact that being passionate about something will mean subordinating other things in her life, it is clear that Kathy had not considered this before. It makes sense to consider the ecological effects of taking on the Ability before acquiring it in order to be sure that it is going to make changes in your world that you are wanting and willing to make.

2. Connect having the Ability to satisfying one of your Prime Motivators.

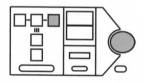 Whatever the model requires of you, it is undoubtedly something unfamiliar and new (otherwise you would probably already be doing it). Left to our own devices we tend to respond in ways that are familiar to us. This simple behavioral fact can provide a sufficiently high bump in the road to hinder the implementation of even the most innocuous, easily grasped model. Acquiring even simple abilities requires a Motivating Cause-Effect capable of providing sufficient motivation for you to make the effort to satisfy the Criterion.

Building the experiences/connections that make up an Ability is like building a tower to get a good view. When you lay the first bricks you do not get the better view; knowing that eventually you will get that view is what keeps you building. Similarly, you need a compelling motivation for learning the Ability in order to carry you through the clumsy period of acquisition. The Motivating Cause-Effect makes it personally worth the time and effort needed to become competent at the Ability.

The "Motivator" in the Motivating Cause-Effect, then, needs to be something that is intrinsically important to *you*, that is, one that is a *Prime*

Motivator. For this reason, the Motivator is the one element in the Array that we suggest you *not* adopt from your exemplar. For example, what makes "Being Appreciative" so important to Kendall is that it leads to "Loving and being loved." Loving and being loved are undoubtedly experiences that Kathy enjoys and cares about, as well. But in her experience it does not occupy the same central role as it does in Kendall's. What *does* have that same oomph for Kathy is, "We women discover we are *all* beautiful." That is her Prime Motivator in the context of her business. By connecting "Being Appreciative" to fulfilling "We women discover we are *all* beautiful," being appreciative (and its attendant strategies and behaviors) becomes important to pursue. (Of course, if by chance your exemplar's Prime Motivator is one that you share, great. We are not suggesting that yours has to be different, only that it has to be personally compelling.)

As demonstrated in the DVD, the way to identify your Prime Motivator is to begin by asking yourself "Why is it important to be able to [Ability]?" (For example, imagine you are acquiring the ability to easily recall the names of people you meet. You would ask, "Why is it important to be able to easily recall peoples' names?" Let's say that your answer is, "So I can use their name when I speak with them.") You then ask yourself, "Why is [previous answer] important?" (In our example, "Why is using their name when I speak with them important?" And your answer might be, "Because that is part of being respectful of them.") You repeatedly ask yourself, "why is [previous answer] important?" until you get to the point that:

* You realize there is nothing beyond your last answer (that your last answer *is* your Prime Motivator), or…

* You are coming up with apparently different answers that are actually the same answer phrased in different ways (you have actually been restating your Prime Motivator in different ways), or…

* You are justifying your answer with explanations such as, "Well, it just *is*," "What else *is* there?" or "That's just what life is *about*" (because your own Prime Motivator is likely to seem self-evident or obviously true).

Once you know your Prime Motivator, find reference experiences that demonstrate to you that having the Ability you have modeled can contribute to fulfilling your Prime Motivator. Like taking on any new cause-effect (or any new belief), once you have made this connection your new cause-effect will orient you to notice and fish out of your experiences more and more examples that support that connection. For example, in working with Kathy, we helped her recognize how being passionate about her work supports (connects to) "We women discover we are *all* beautiful."

3. Identify a PAST SITUATION in which you *really needed* the Ability.

In several of the following acquisition steps you will be accessing the various elements of the Array and practicing them in imagination. By identifying ahead of time an actual, personal situation in which having the Ability would have made a significant difference, you provide yourself with a relevant example that you can immediately step into. Having an actual situation within which to test the elements also creates an opportunity to experience how manifesting the Ability *does* make a significant difference in how you respond in such situations (further supporting the connection between having the Ability and satisfying your Prime Motivator).

4. Access the Criterion/Definition/Evidence and the Sustaining Emotion, then step into the PAST SITUATION while holding those elements in your experience. Practice this until you can access them easily.

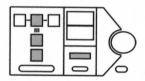

a) *Access Criterion/Definition:* Since everything in the Array is happening in relation to the Criterion, that is where to begin acquisition. (If you instead begin with the Strategy, the internal processes and external behaviors are likely to seem fuzzy and irrelevant because you have not first established what it is that you are wanting to satisfy or fulfill—the Criterion—through thinking and behaving in those ways.) However, it is not advisable to simply reach into your own experience for the exemplar's Criterion. The word your exemplar uses as the label for her Criterion may mean something different to you than it does to her. You need to use your exemplar's meaning, and this is given in her Definition. Therefore, you will need to access the Criterion and Definition together, as one thing. That is, you begin by searching through your personal history for reference experiences for the Criterion *as Defined in the model.*

You may already have in your ocean of experience references for the Criterion-Definition connection made by your exemplar. Even if you do not, you will almost certainly have examples of the *kind of experience* your exemplar defines as her Criterion, just labeled differently. In that case, establish a new connection for yourself by first accessing your own reference experiences for the *exemplar's* Definition, and then recognize that *those* experiences are what is meant by the exemplar's Criterion. For example, your exemplar's Criterion/Definition is: "Success" *means* "Attaining the goals I set for myself." For you, however, the meaning of Success has been, "Doing better than anyone expected." Even so, you probably have examples of *attaining goals you had set for yourself.* Access *those* reference experiences and see (re-label) them as "Successes." (This is the approach that was taken with Kathy on the DVD.)

b) *Access Evidence:* Once you know on what to focus your attention (the Criterion/Definition), you can add in the experiential signals—the Evidence— that let you know when that Criterion is being satisfied. Once again, retrieve your personal reference experiences for seeing, hearing, or feeling the kinds of things that serve as Evidence for the Criterion.

c) *Access Sustaining Emotion:* Because the Sustaining Emotion *holds in the body* many of the essential relationships that are held in the beliefs, accessing the Sustaining Emotion now will help you hold the Criterion in your experience as you practice manifesting the Ability in your imagination. Depending upon the Sustaining Emotion, you may be able to access it directly. If this is difficult, range through your personal history until you find an instance—even a momentary one—when you felt that emotion. Recapture that reference experience, making it more and more vivid and intense, until you can easily maintain the Sustaining Emotion.

d) *Step into the* PAST SITUATION: Once you can access the Criterion/Definition/Evidence and Sustaining Emotion, step into the past situation while holding those elements in your experience. Repeat stepping in and out of that past situation until you can easily access the Criterion, Definition, Evidence, and Sustaining Emotion. Be sure to notice how operating through this Criterion and Sustaining Emotion contributes to your being able to manifest the Ability in that situation.

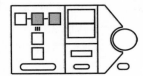

Also, as you begin to manifest the Ability, notice the ways in which your responses change, *and also the way those new responses usefully affect the situation.* Use this recognition to further **recognize that, when you satisfy the Criterion, you are also helping to satisfy your Prime Motivator.**

5. Access reference experiences for any Supporting Beliefs, and take them into the PAST SITUATION.

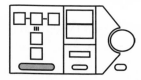

You almost certainly already have experiences in your personal history that can serve as references for the Supporting Beliefs of the Ability. Retrieve reference experiences until you find the one (or enough of them) that makes the Supporting Belief become something you recognize as true. Then step into the context of the Ability and notice how that Belief supports you in manifesting the Ability.

6. Take the Primary Strategy and External Behaviors into the PAST SITUATION, and practice them until they are working for you.

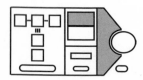

A strategy is a blend of internal processes and external behaviors. The behaviors specified in the Primary Strategy do not operate independently of those specified in External Behavior, but in concert with them. It is the combined action of all of these behaviors that help make it possible to manifest the Ability (and to fulfill the Criterion). (Remember that the purpose of establishing a separate box for External Behaviors was to draw our attention *during elicitation* to those behaviors that are essential and that might not automatically manifest themselves.) Therefore, when it comes to acquisition, we include the External Behaviors in the process of acquiring the Primary Strategy.

Take yourself through the steps of the Strategy, making sure that you can access—do—each of them. If a particular step is either unfamiliar or difficult for you to do, find a reference experience in your personal history for doing it. (This is what we did with Kathy as she acquired each of the three sub-Strategies that make up Kendall's Primary Strategy.)

You may be able to facilitate acquisition by finding the Primary Strategy already intact somewhere in your experience. It is possible that there is some context in your life in which you already use the same patterns of thinking and behaving as those in the Primary Strategy. For example, you might discover that the strategy your stock trader exemplar uses to pick good trades is essentially the same strategy you use in selecting gifts for your family. These two contexts are very different in terms of their content: trades for the stock market; gifts for the family. Even so, the form of the internal processes and external behaviors for these two contexts might be (for you) very much the same. If you can find such a strategy match, that familiar context can serve as a reference experience for the Primary Strategy. This will make it much easier to access the Strategy when you step into the context in which you want to manifest the Ability.

Whether you already have an intact reference experience for the Primary Strategy, or need to build up your familiarity with it a step at a time, once you do have access, step into the PAST SITUATION and practice the Primary Strategy. (As you do, be sure to continue to hold the Criterion in your awareness. It is, after all, what the Strategy and Behavior are working to satisfy.)

7. Recognize that the Enabling Cause-Effect is _true_.

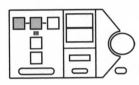

The Enabling Cause-Effect expresses your exemplar's beliefs regarding what leads to or makes possible having her Criterion satisfied. The Enabling Cause-Effect reflects what is happening in parts of the Strategy. Therefore, your experiences with stepping in, running the Primary Strategy, and satisfying the Criterion will have provided you with _personal_ examples demonstrating the causal connection between the Enabling Cause and the Criterion.

8. Practice the entire Ability in _other_ past situations, until you are sure that you can easily access the elements.

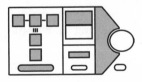

Now that you are familiar with almost all of the elements of the Array, you can practice accessing and using them in past situations _other_ than the one you have been using in the previous steps. It is best if these additional practice situations are also ones in which you would have liked to have had the Ability that you are acquiring, so that you can really notice the difference made by manifesting the Ability.

9. Think of any real-world difficulties that could arise (difficulties that could stop you from manifesting the Ability), and practice overcoming them by using the Secondary Strategies.

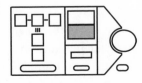

Anyone can be proficient when the world cooperates, responding just as we want it to. When we practice in imagination, we tend to imagine things going smoothly, and this does not fully prepare us for real life, which is not always so accommodating. One of the qualities that makes someone an exemplar is that their Ability is robust. That is, they are able to respond effectively regardless of the monkey wrenches that the world might throw into the works.

While the world will always provide surprises, for the most part we have pretty accurate ideas about what can go wrong in a particular situation. An important part of acquisition is to throw as many of those potential monkey wrenches into the works as you can, and then discover ways to usefully respond to them. This makes your Ability more robust and resilient.

As with the Primary Operation, first make sure that you can access the repertoire of internal processes and external behaviors called for in the Secondary Operations. Then step into a PAST SITUATION, imagine each of those difficulties (the monkey wrenches) happening, and address them with the Secondary Operations until you are comfortable with the outcome.

10. Identify the next time you will need the Ability, and rehearse manifesting it in that situation.

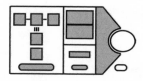

Up to this point, all of the practicing you have been doing has been in the context of *past* situations in which you could have used your newly acquired Ability. This is useful for becoming familiar with it. The final step in the *access* stage of acquisition is to rehearse manifesting the Ability in a future situation in which you will want to use it. This not only provides you with more practice, but it helps anchor the Ability into that situation, and will make using it for the first time in the real world more familiar and less threatening.

Contributing Factors

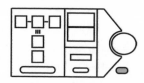

Now that you are familiar with everything that is *within* the Array, you are in a position to incorporate any Contributing Factors. While not essential to manifesting the Ability, Contributing Factors nevertheless can provide significant support for it. For instance, earlier we used as an example the ability to prepare for exams, for which the exemplar had as a Contributing Factor, "Make sure I get sufficient sleep the night before." Other examples of factors contributing to an Ability could be, "Gather information on particular financial markets," or "Have a storehouse of humorous stories," or "Convey a feeling of security to those you work with by having your office paneled in dark wood." The variety of possible Contributing Factors is endless. In terms of acquisition, consider adding them to your repertoire to the extent that you want to and can.

Integration: Becoming Competent

Beware of bugs in the above code;
I have only proved it correct, not tried it.

Donald Knuth, computer scientist

We cannot model the full depth and breadth of the experiential connections that the exemplar has acquired during years of manifesting their particular Ability. There will always be more to an Ability than is captured in our model of it. For the exemplar, years of manifesting her Ability in the real world has developed in her innumerable layers of experience, each of which includes intricate webs of minute and unconscious perceptions and behaviors. If we want to be competent (and eventually proficient—that is, exemplars ourselves of the Ability), we need to establish that same depth and breadth of experience in ourselves. What we can model—and want to acquire—is the structure that makes all that *possible*.

True competency comes from *using* the structure in the real world. No amount of rehearsal and monkey wrenching will provide you with experiences as rich as those you get in the real world. In that richness are the opportunities to really exercise the muscles of your model, to integrate it more and more thoroughly with who you are, and to learn the countless subtleties that will make you proficient at the Ability.

Of course, you will make mistakes. But what is a mistake? A dusty childhood memory of one of the authors: In the 60's, Professor Julius Sumner Miller conducted a weekly television show on physics called, "Why Is It So?" As a teacher, Miller was fiery and crusty...and passionate. He always had several high school students sitting beside his lab bench to harangue, and the rest of us eavesdropped from our homes. In one particularly memorable show, he ran an experiment that did not go at all as he said it would. In a flash he turned on the students and barked, "Okay, what happened?! What happened?!" One of the students sputtered, "The experiment failed." Miller scowled at the student wrathfully and said, "An experiment *never* fails! There is always a result!" And then he smiled and said, "In fact, you will learn more from those experiments that don't turn out the way you expected them to."

Few of us enjoy making mistakes: if we make enough of them—or even just one doozy—the whole enterprise can quickly become daunting and make giving up seem attractive. Nevertheless, those mistakes are opportunities to learn, to recalibrate, and to extend our grasp to include yet more of the subtleties of the Ability. Responding to mistakes and difficulties as opportunities to learn is fundamental to perseverance, and persevering through the initial fumbling period during which you are making the model your own is essential in making the Ability your own.

Hindrances

Acquisition is a process of both familiarizing yourself with the model and integrating its structure into your own experience. Notice, we did not say "adding" its structure, but "*integrating*." You are not an empty vessel to be filled with the structure of the model. Nor are you clay just waiting to be gripped and molded by it. You are, in a sense, already full of you; you already have form. When you take on a new Ability—acquire a model—remember that *there is already someone there*: you.

In using the metaphor "someone is already there," we are not suggesting that there is only so much room in each one of us for experience. Experience is infinitely elastic and endlessly capable of incorporating new elements. There is always room for change.

The ease of acquiring a particular Ability depends both upon the Ability and upon you. It is not determined by whether the Ability involves only a few, simple patterns or involves many elements (like Kendall's ability to be passionate). Ease of acquisition depends upon whether or not the model is asking you to do something that is either very foreign to your previous experiences or conflicts with beliefs you already have. Foreign or conflicting elements of the Ability are *hindrances*, not brick walls. Unlike a brick wall, running into one of these hindrances simply means that you need to do some extra work to be able to continue on. Any hindrance you might run into will probably be one of the following three types:

No Reference Experience

It can happen that a model asks you to take on a belief, an emotion, a way of thinking or of behaving for which you have no compelling reference experiences. For instance, in the DVD demonstration of Kathy acquiring the ability to be passionate, we see that she does not have readily accessible reference experiences for how perceiving details can enhance her being appreciative. David arranges an experience for her to have that can serve as a reference:

David: Here, I'll give you an example. [pointing] There's your glass with a little bit of tea left in it, right? So, you look at that glass... What do you think of that glass? Just look at it.

Kathy: Uh, it's blue.

David: It's blue. It's a glass. No big deal, right?

Kathy: Right.

David: Now I want you to look at it and start noticing reflections...little areas of light...how the blue changes—

Kathy: [smiling] Right.

David: —where it's dark...where it's shiny—

Kathy: Right.

David: Where it glistens...the edges and shape. And just start noticing more and more details. Find out how your experience changes in relation to it.

Kathy: [laughs] It's actually quite pretty!

If you do not already have a reference experience that makes a particular element of the Array come alive, it means you need to somehow arrange to have that experience. You can have someone help you do that, as Kathy did, or you can arrange to have a needed experience on your own. For example, suppose that the model you are acquiring requires that you "be open to the world of another person," but this is not something you are familiar with. You could (for instance) arrange to spend some time on the floor with a child, learning to play in her world, as a way of giving yourself the reference experience.

Belief Conflict

It can happen that there is a conflict between an element of experience prescribed in the model and one of your closely held beliefs. For instance, again supposing that the model requires you to "be open to the world of another person," perhaps you believe that if you are open to someone, "that person can control me." Though conflicts like this often feel insurmountable at first, they can usually be resolved through reframing, that is, by seeing things from a different perspective.

An example of resolving a belief conflict in the work with Kathy comes when she responds with obvious disbelief to the notion that she could possibly do all of the complex things that are being presented to her in the model:

Kathy: This is all going on in my brain in just the short moment I'm speaking to this person?

David: Oh yeah—

Kathy: Hah! [laughs derisively]

David: —No problem. Now right now, of course, it's *not* going on in your brain.

Kathy: No.

David: It's going on out here. [pointing to chart]

Kathy: Oh. Okay.

David: So it's slow. It seems like, Oh my god, this is forever!

David then uses the reference experience of learning to write to give Kathy a more useful way to think about what she is doing. Kathy ends up relaxed and nodding, and observes, "So we're altering my thinking." She had been thinking of the Array as something to *know*, as in knowing information. David reframed it as something to *learn*, which involves a growing familiarity over time. This was fine with her.

Unwanted Consequences

Probably no Ability—or aspect of an Ability—is appropriate for all situations. As you imagine using the new Ability you might discover that it creates an unwanted consequence. That is, manifesting the Ability leads to something happening that you would not like, or is not appropriate, or is not useful. An unwanted consequence does not mean you have to give up the Ability, however, only that you need to *contextualize* it.

To contextualize is to create boundaries around a particular situation. For example, being at work and being at home are probably different situations (contexts) for you. Each of these contexts can be divided into smaller contexts, as well. At home, you may have it that "free time for myself" is a different context than "being with my partner," and so on.

An example of an unwanted consequence came up with Kathy shortly after her initial acquisition work with David. She found herself using the Strategy for being passionate when she was with someone who she really did not like and who treated her badly. Not only was it difficult to manifest the Strategy under those circumstances, she did not think it was even a good idea to appreciate and enjoy this person. We agreed and helped her to re-contextualize the Strategy by drawing a boundary around "people who treat me badly" as a context in which it is not appropriate to manifest her ability to be passionate.

* * *

We recognize that the personal work required to access a needed reference experience, resolve a belief conflict, or appropriately contextualize an Ability may, in some cases, be considerable. If you run into a hindrance that you cannot get past by yourself, we suggest getting help from someone who is skilled at personal change work.

Afterword

Human cultures have always found ways to pass on their accumulated wisdom to future generations. We transmit what things to do and how to do them through oral tradition, social rules, rites, rituals, writing and, more recently, through the recording of voice and image. Today, the learning of certain abilities is seen as so crucial to cultural survival that formal education is now mandatory in many countries. For these reasons alone, the process of modeling as a formal technique for replicating human abilities is clearly something of great practical use, and worthy of further development.

The significance of modeling is much greater than that, however. The *idea* of modeling is itself something that can take us far beyond the utility of individuals acquiring specific desirable abilities. Suppose that modeling became an idea utterly woven into what is culturally and socially accepted in the same way as we now accept as a given that everyone is entitled to equal protection under the law. Once it is generally assumed that it is possible to model the desirable abilities of others, and to then make those models available to anyone, personal and societal notions about what is possible to change will necessarily transform in some fundamental ways. Few people would be asking "Can I do this?" Instead they would be asking "*How* can I do this?" That is a very different question, one that presumes capability. Instead of unnecessarily accepting limitations, the question "How can I do this?" recasts as a matter of *choice* our pursuit of personal and professional expressions, contributions, and fulfillments.

We need not be concerned that an abundance of choice will lead to a homogeneous—and therefore boring—world. Because of the infinite variety of our personal histories and life experiences, different people will make different choices regarding which abilities they want to acquire. Furthermore, any two—or two hundred—individuals manifesting the same ability will nevertheless express that ability in different ways. Each of them will express that ability *through* their own, unique personalities; not in spite of them. Indeed, it is our belief that making widely available the models for developing a vast array of human abilities would create many more opportunities to tap and bring into the world the unique potentials latent inside every one of us.

Furthermore, as familiarity with modeling grows, so too will our appreciation for the uniqueness of those around us. There is more to the uniqueness of every person on the planet than just his or her thumb print. Each of us also represents a unique web of life experiences, the threads of which have braided into a singular personality, an individual with characteristic, peculiar, and amazing perceptions, talents, and abilities. There are many wonderful violinists, many people are good at telling jokes, many can relax easily, can write a good letter, or can power through a complex task. And yet, no two of these wonderful violinists will approach their music and play in exactly the same way. And when one of these wonderful violinists is gone, her particular approach to music is gone as well. Similarly, no two humorists will tell their tales the same way. And there are many ways of relaxing, of writing a good letter, and of powering through tasks. Modeling makes it possible to capture the workings of a particular ability *as well as* some of the unique attributes of a particular individual's way of manifesting that ability. Those idiosyncratic and fortuitous attributes may themselves prove to be a revelation, affording us a depth and range of experience and capability that would otherwise remain unavailable.

In this book we have engaged in an enterprise biologist/epistemologist Dr. Francisco Varela described as "laying down a path in walking." Together we have taken a few steps in laying down a path in the terrain of human experience. We have created this particular path of modeling by walking it into this book. That path leads to many possible futures, any one of which can only be brought forth by our continuing to walk it, individually and collectively. The full exploration of this beautiful and surprising land has begun.

We have quite a stroll ahead of us.

Appendices

I.   Good Questions

II.   Experiential Array: Elicitation Definitions

III. Experiential Array: Elicitation Questions

IV.   Example Array: Lenny

Appendix I: Good Questions

How can I get a better sense of—and get better at—"stepping in"?

Asking questions is an active and intentional attempt to understand the exemplar from *inside* her experience. Stepping in is how we get inside the exemplar's experience. Here are some suggestions for how to better access in your experience and behavior the elements of stepping in:

* RECOGNIZE THAT EXPERIENCE HAS STRUCTURE AND THAT, THEREFORE, YOU NEED TO LEARN HOW TO THINK, FEEL AND BEHAVE AS THE EXEMPLAR DOES:

    Taking on and being affected by other people's structure is not an exotic notion, but a fact of experience. You have benefited countless times from other people sharing with you some aspect of their experiential world. It could have been something you read, heard in a movie, were told by a friend, or overheard on a bus. Regardless of where it came from, that tidbit of behavior or different way of thinking about the world changed how you understood and responded to the world from that point on.

    Take some time to identify examples of times when the structure of your thinking changed (though you may not have recognized it at the time) and, so, caused your experience and behavior to change as well. It is important to find enough real examples to convince yourself that a new understanding does indeed change the structure of your thinking and, so, your experience as well.

* OPEN YOURSELF TO THE EXEMPLAR'S EXPERIENCE:

    Create space in your own internal experience for that of the exemplar. It is through being open that you get the greatest chance to have empathetic access to the experience of your exemplar. Although we are sure you already have reference experiences of this, they may have gone unnoticed by you. Let us suggest a few that you might recognize:

    • Getting down on the floor to play with a child (*not* to entertain the child, but to be *with* the child in her world).

- Standing before an awe-inspiring landscape.

- Being with someone you love and soaking up that person, noticing and appreciating how she moves, the sound of her voice, what she says, the play of expressions, and so on.

- Being whisked into a theme ride at an amusement park, and giving yourself over to the world of puppetry and painted plaster.

- Entering the impossible world created by a movie fantasy.

- Meditation.

- Listening to a close friend who is hurting and needs to be heard, without judgment and without feeling you have to solve the problem.

- Being in the presence of a respected and admired mentor as she or he is teaching you what they know (like a grandfather showing you how to use tools, or a professor teaching you how to identify a butterfly).

Re-connect with personal reference experiences such as these to give yourself a more immediate sense of the state of being open.

* *FEEL REVERENCE FOR THIS PERSON:*

When we speak of "reverence" we mean appreciating and honoring this person's experience as something which is unique, valuable, hard won, and inseparable from the person herself. Reverence is a feeling of deep respect for someone (or something) plus the added quality of awe.

Think of several people you know (or know of) toward whom you feel reverence until you create for yourself a solid sense of what that reverence feels like. If you are having difficulty finding examples, begin with something or someplace toward which you feel reverence. Once you have that feeling well in hand (body), search for a time when you felt the same way toward a person. As you begin to work with your exemplar, recognize that she has something unique and special to offer—just like those special people in your own life—and recapture that feeling of reverence.

* *WHAT TO DO:*

1. Either sit or stand at the same level as your exemplar (or below).

This helps the exemplar feel at ease, and you will find it easier to step into her experience as well.

2. Get a description of the context in which she manifests her Ability, that is, the who, what, where, and when. This gives you the world of the exemplar to step into as you gather information, and is essential to understanding the significance of what you are learning. (The words "I see red" will be understood differently if the contextual world is "My wife is criticizing me," than if it is "I'm planning a painting" or "I'm at a family gathering...Hey, there's Uncle Red!")

3. While the exemplar is responding to a question, become very still and quiet inside, and devote your full attention to her. Your stillness will support your exemplar in feeling free to explore her own experience, avoids distracting her with your own responses, and allows you to more easily and precisely feel the effect of her description of experience as you take it on yourself (that is, as you step in).

4. Let the exemplar's description take over your body, using the exemplar's words to guide your experience:

   • Things she says, say to yourself (internally or externally).

   • Things she describes seeing or feeling, see and feel for yourself.

   • Feel in your body what you see her doing with her body (especially anything unusual, characteristic, or exaggerated).

   • Shift your body (breathing, facial expression, movements) as necessary in order to "try on" the experience.

   • It is not the words themselves but the dynamics they create in your experience that are important. Your ongoing question is "How does this affect my experience?"

5. Check the accuracy of your stepping in by describing your understanding and experience to your exemplar.

What do I do when I have difficulty stepping into my exemplar's experience?

Consider, "Have I opened myself enough to this person's experience?" If not, empty yourself of the structure you have been trying to take on and shift your body posture (move around, stretch, change your breathing). Again access a personal reference experience of being open (as we described above). Then resume taking on in your own experience each element of your exemplar's structure, checking each one with your exemplar to make sure you understand it. You may also want to re-elicit an element of experience that is difficult for you to step into. This time, however, ask about it in a different way in order to (hopefully) elicit a description that is more effective in helping you to take on that element.

What should I do when the exemplar's answer does not fit the question I asked?

The standard elicitation questions have proven themselves effective in orienting the exemplar to the precise information you are after. Even so, there are no guarantees that your exemplar will make sense out of them in the way you intended. Words compel experience, but this does not mean that they will compel the experience of everyone in the same way, or in a way that is completely predictable. Meaning is not in the words themselves, but is ascribed to those words by the person using (or responding to) them. Your exemplar will answer the question *as she understands it*. Therefore, it is important to do your best to ask your question in a way likely to take your exemplar down the experiential path you need her to explore.

For example, suppose we are modeling an architect and want to know what her thoughts are while designing a home. We could ask "What are you feeling when you are designing a home?" This question asks her to identify her *feelings*. But we want to know what she is *thinking*, so it is more useful and appropriate to ask "What are you thinking when you are designing a home?" This is a fairly obvious example, but your exemplar will respond to the subtlest aspects of your questions, as well. Suppose we ask the architect the following two questions:

"What are you thinking when designing a home?"

"What are you thinking about when designing a home?"

Both questions may seem to be asking the exemplar to go down the same experiential path, that is, identifying what she is thinking when designing a home. But take a moment to ask those two questions of yourself. You will discover that they take you down different paths. The first question orients you more to being *in* the act of designing a home and pulls your thoughts from that perspective, while the second question puts you more in the observer role. In other words, the first question asks the exemplar for an *ongoing report* of what is happening in her thinking, while the "about" in the second question suggests *analyzing* what she is thinking when designing a home.

If the question you have used is not helping your exemplar access the information you need, you need to be flexible and creative in finding another way to ask for the information. The most important advice we can give you when it comes to generating questions is to keep in mind just what *kind* of information you are asking for. For instance, if you want to elicit your exemplar's Motivating Cause-Effect, be clear in your own mind about what a Motivating Cause-Effect *is* before asking your questions. This will not only help you formulate an appropriate question, but it will also help you recognize whether or not your exemplar's response is an answer to *that* question, or is about some other aspect of her experience.

Is there an ideal sequence for elicitation?

There are no right or wrong sequences for eliciting the elements of the Experiential Array. Nevertheless, there is a sequence we have found that usually works well, one that we try to follow: Criterion, Definition, Evidence, Enabling Cause-Effect, Motivating Cause-Effect, Primary Strategy, Secondary Strategies, Sustaining Emotion and, finally, External Behavior.

This sequence emerged from our experiences in elicitation. For most people, the flow of this sequence is natural and logical:

Everything operates in relation to the Criterion, so identifying the Criterion first makes sure you are at the *heart* of the Ability.

↳ The Definition is a refinement of the Criterion, and Evidence is a refinement of both of them.

↳ It is easier to correctly identify Enabling and Motivating Cause-Effects once you have identified the Criterion (Definition and Evidence) that is being enabled and motivated.

↳ In a sense, the Primary Strategy operates to bring to life the world of relationships described by the Belief Template. So having the Belief Template first helps focus the exemplar on the relevant Strategy.

↳ The Secondary Strategies engage when the Primary Strategy is not sufficient.

↳ The Sustaining Emotion is often quite subtle and, so, may not have been as much in the exemplar's awareness as the other elements. Eliciting the Beliefs and Strategies before the Sustaining Emotion helps bring the awareness of the exemplar more fully into the experience of her Ability, and so makes her more able to notice her Sustaining Emotion.

↳ External Behavior is saved for last since we want to identify only those behaviors that are unique to the ability *and* are not likely to emerge automatically from the Beliefs, Strategies, and Emotions. By specifying these other elements first, we help the exemplar narrow the field of External Behaviors to those that are significant.

What should I do if my exemplar wants to begin (or I want to begin) with something other than her Criterion?

For reasons explained above, we try to begin by *planting our flag* in the Criterion and explore from there. To plant the flag is to find something about the structure of the exemplar's experience that you are confident *does* belong to the Ability. You expand your subsequent information gathering from that "flag."

Using the architect as an example, we could plant our flag in her External Behavior of walking around the property. With that as our point of reference, we can then move on to the Criterion by asking something like "As you are walking around the property, what is important to you?" In effect, we are asking her "What Criterion is that External Behavior intended to help satisfy?"

In fact you can plant the flag anywhere in the Array and set off from that point, *as long as you continue to test each new piece of information for its "fit" with the rest of the Array*. The ongoing question you are asking yourself is: "Does this fit with what else is operating in the Array, or not?" This test keeps you focused on what is relevant and what, though interesting, is nevertheless outside of the Array in focus. You can plant your flag anywhere in the Array as long as you make sure that the Array grows into a coherent whole. So, if your sense during elicitation is to begin with, say, External Behavior (because it is easier, or it is what the exemplar wants to talk about, or something about it captures your interest), then plant your flag there.

I'm finding the same or similar descriptions of elements in different areas of the Array. Is this okay?

It is not only okay, it is something you can expect to find. The elements of an Array—and of an Ability—have a special relationship with each other: they all *fit* with each other. Beliefs, Strategies, Emotions, and External Behaviors are, in a sense, different languages that are being used to describe *one* thing. You will therefore find patterns that are common to some of the elements *and* patterns that are unique to only one element.

When I compare my exemplar's three examples, one of them is missing some of the information that seems to be true for the other two. Does that mean the third example is not a good one and I need to have her find another?

Suppose we are modeling our exemplar's ability to forgive. In her first example she mentions that she experienced humor while forgiving someone, but says nothing about humor when she describes her second example of forgiveness. The fact that humor was not mentioned in the second example does not mean it was not there. Instead, she may have simply omitted it in her description. Or perhaps the gravity of the second situation overshadowed the humor, but it was there nonetheless, though in a muted and brief form. Or perhaps the exemplar feels a bit embarrassed to admit that she was finding humor in an obviously serious situation. There can be any number of reasons and factors that prevent a particular element from surfacing into awareness (or description) in a particular example.

The difference between the two examples may also be just a matter of language. The richness of language makes it possible to express the same ideas in endless ways. It is true that different words for the same thing will convey subtle differences. But those subtle differences may or may not be significant to your exemplar. For instance, being "delighted" and being "pleased" may be distinctly different experiences for you, but for your exemplar, being "delighted" and being "pleased" may be much the same experience, and so she uses them interchangeably.

Separating apparent differences (omissions and individual uses of language) from actual differences is often as simple as asking your exemplar "Are these the same, or are they in fact different?" You will probably see your exemplar flip back and forth between them as she compares the two experiences. Almost always, your exemplar will resolve the discrepancy, either by filling in what was omitted, or by explaining that they are different descriptions for the same experience, or by confirming that they are indeed different experiences.

What do I do if I identify actual differences between the examples?

Filling in omissions and resolving discrepancies in description will not account for all of the differences between the examples. Some of those differences will, in fact, be differences. Not all differences matter. Some of those actual differences will be idiosyncratic to the particular situation surrounding an example and, therefore, irrelevant to the structure of the Ability itself. For instance, suppose our exemplar of the ability to forgive describes forgiving an adult in one example and forgiving a child in another. That is an actual difference between the two examples. If, however, "it just happened to be an adult in one and a child in the other," then it is not a difference that is significant in terms of manifesting the ability to forgive, and you can ignore it.

Another possibility is that the reason you are finding real differences between examples is that one of the examples is actually not an example of what you want to model. For instance, we might discover that our exemplar of forgiveness was not actually forgiving the child in that example, but simply being tolerant. In this case, you need to set it aside by explaining to your exemplar how it is *not* an example of the Ability you are interested in. Then have her find another. The contrast of the not-quite-right one will help her easily identify another example that is just what you want.

A third possibility is that the differences between examples reveals that you do not have the Ability appropriately defined. For example, if it turns out that forgiving a child *is* different from forgiving an adult, then you need to decide if you are going to model forgiving children, or forgiving adults, or forgiving in general. In such a case, make sure that you appropriately re-focus both you *and* the exemplar by using the different examples to more accurately define the Ability you want to model.

When would I want to model several exemplars for the same ability?

If you want to do something the way a particular exemplar does it, you only need to model that person. However, you may want a *generic model*. A generic model emerges from comparing the Arrays of several exemplars for the same Ability. The result is a model that leaves out the idiosyncrasies of an individual exemplar and instead preserves only the structure common to *anyone* who effectively manifests the Ability.

If you are creating a model that you want to make available to people besides yourself (through books, programs, seminars, etc.), it may be a good idea to go after a generic model. Because the across-exemplar comparison strips out the individual idiosyncrasies, the final model will be simpler. It will have only the essential elements of the Ability and, so, will be simpler to present and easier for you to create group acquisition experiences.

If you decide to create a generic model you need to compare and contrast at least three exemplars. This comparison will make obvious the idiosyncrasies of each exemplar. These idiosyncratic patterns can be set aside, leaving only those patterns that are operating in the Ability for all of your exemplars. The process of patterning across exemplars is much the same as that of patterning across examples. You are still searching for that which is the same among the exemplars, and resolving the differences through recovering omitted information and through working out discrepancies between their descriptions.

For example, after modeling Kendall, we modeled Terry, who also has the ability to be passionate about something, though his passion is for playing soccer. Although there are differences between his model and Kendall's, there are also striking similarities. For instance, both of them hold a Big Picture that has the quality of a "dream," both put thoughts into action, both tell people about what they are experiencing in relation to their passions, and both feel excitement that cycles with another, intensifying emotion (for Kendall this is "Grateful," for Terry it is "Fully Alive"). Finding these similarities suggests that they may be generic; that is, they are patterns of the ability to be passionate about something *for anyone.*

When patterning across exemplars, however, discrepencies can become more marked and complicated to resolve. This is because each exemplar will have his or her own ways of describing the patterns of experience that they nonetheless share. (For example, Kendall talked about "holding the *big* picture," while Terry talked about "holding the *broader* picture.") The patterns you discover are not likely to be expressed by the exemplars in exactly the same words and phrases. (Though this *does* happen on occasion; both Kendall and Terry described their Sustaining Emotion as "Excited.") At some point after you have finished with the elicitations you will have to make your own decisions about what words and descriptions effectively capture and convey the *shared patterns of experience* you found in your exemplars.

When I am refining the model, is it okay to leave out some of the elements that the exemplar described?

We have encouraged you to respect and hold as almost sacred your exemplar's description of her experience, to keep it in her words, rather than transform it into your interpretation of her experience. Throughout elicitation our allegiance has been to the world of the exemplar as we try to answer the question, "What *must* be operating in the structure of the exemplar's experience for her to be manifesting this Ability?"

When you are setting forth the model for your *own* use, however, that allegiance is over. *Your allegiance is now to the model alone,* and the question becomes, "What elements of that structure do I need to take on in order to manifest this ability?"

It may not be necessary to take on all of the rich details and nuances of perception, thought, and behavior that you have captured in the boxes of the Array. To identify what is *essential* for you to be able to take on the Ability:

1. Step into manifesting the Ability, holding as much of the Array as you can in your experience.

2. Put your attention on the different experiential elements one at a time, and ask yourself, "How does this affect my experience in this context?" That is, identify how each experiential element affects your ability to continue to manifest the Ability.

3. If there are any elements which seem to have little or no effect on you, drop them from your experience. Do you still get the full expression of the Ability?

If you can still manifest the Ability without explicitly accessing a particular pattern, then that pattern is unnecessary. Eliminating unnecessary patterns from your model will probably make your model easier to acquire. But be careful not to eliminate something simply because you think you do not need it, or because you do not like it; the test of what is essential can only be made through the direct experience of *using* it.

When it comes to acquisition, how can I increase the chances of an experience being strong enough to become a reference experience?

There are many factors that can affect how compelling an experience is and, so, how likely it is to become a reference experience. Some of these are that the experience:

*   Supports your self-concept

- Connects with core criteria ("values")
- Comes from a credible/authoritative source (person, book, etc.)
- Resolves a felt need or vexing question
- Is surprising
- Generates intense feelings (pleasant or unpleasant)
- Makes sense

For example, suppose one evening you decide to take a walk in the neighborhood instead of watching television. You have a pleasant walk, chat with a neighbor or two along the way, notice a lovely garden just a block away, and so on. You might return from this walk refreshed and delighted, but unchanged. It remains just one of countless experiences you have had. Suppose instead that you are surprised at the relief you feel at having got away from the television, and notice that you now feel more a part of where you live, which is something you always wanted for yourself. In this second scenario, you might well return from the walk having changed; the walk has become a reference experience for you. This change has happened through the combining effects of (at least) resolving a felt need ("I want to feel more a part of where I live"), surprise, and intense pleasant feelings. All of these possible qualities of a compelling experience are given to the experience by the person having it; there is nothing inherent in any particular experience that necessarily makes it a reference experience. The effect of an experience depends upon the person who is having that experience.

So, if the experience you have accessed is not compelling enough to serve as a reference experience, search again through your personal history for one (or several) that for you has some of the qualities we mention above. That is, look for an experience in which you were surprised, or in which something that was really bothering you was resolved, or in which what happened bolstered your self-concept, and so on.

What do I do when the model asks of me something that seems too difficult or overwhelming?

The way to eat an elephant is one bite at a time. In some cases, a model can be a pretty big elephant to swallow. The difficulty in incorporating a particular model depends on who is doing the eating; different people can take different sized bites. The goal in acquisition is not to take on the model all at once, but to take it on, *period.* So take it on in whatever way suits you best.

No matter how big an experience or behavior may seem at first glance, it can always be chunked down to smaller, constituent elements. For instance, someone who has never danced may have no conceptual or body idea about what to do out on the dance floor. For this person it is an overwhelmingly complex task. Nevertheless, it can be broken down into smaller internal processes and external behaviors. He can begin by simply moving his body to the music. And even this can be chunked down if it proves too difficult. For example, we can have him pick out just the bass line in the music and tap one foot to it. What we are doing is finding this person's *current level of competence,* then building upon that. If you go small enough, you will always find a level of current competency upon which the larger elements of the Ability can be built. This may take some time, but if the Ability is worth having, the investment is one of going slow now, so that you can go fast later on.

Appendix II

Experiential Array: Elicitation Definitions

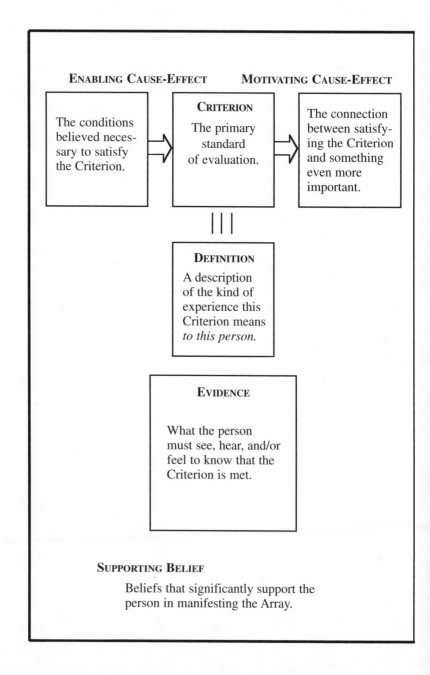

ENABLING CAUSE-EFFECT   MOTIVATING CAUSE-EFFECT

The conditions believed necessary to satisfy the Criterion.

CRITERION

The primary standard of evaluation.

The connection between satisfying the Criterion and something even more important.

DEFINITION

A description of the kind of experience this Criterion means *to this person.*

EVIDENCE

What the person must see, hear, and/or feel to know that the Criterion is met.

SUPPORTING BELIEF

Beliefs that significantly support the person in manifesting the Array.

PRIMARY STRATEGY

The set of internal processes and external behaviors that are usually effective in manifesting the Ability.

SECONDARY STRATEGIES

The internal processes and external behaviors that are engaged when the Primary Strategy is ineffective.

EXTERNAL BEHAVIOR

Those behaviors (movements, facial expressions, verbalizations and voice tonalities) that are significant in manifesting the Ability.

ABILITY

SUSTAINING EMOTION

A background state that helps keep the person actively engaged in manifesting the Ability.

SIGNAL EMOTIONS

Moment-to-moment states that indicate whether or not—or to what degree—the Criterion is currently being satisfied.

CONTRIBUTING FACTORS

Other abilities, prerequisites, preparations, conditions or considerations outside of the Array that significantly support the ability.

Appendix III

Experiential Array: Elicitation Questions

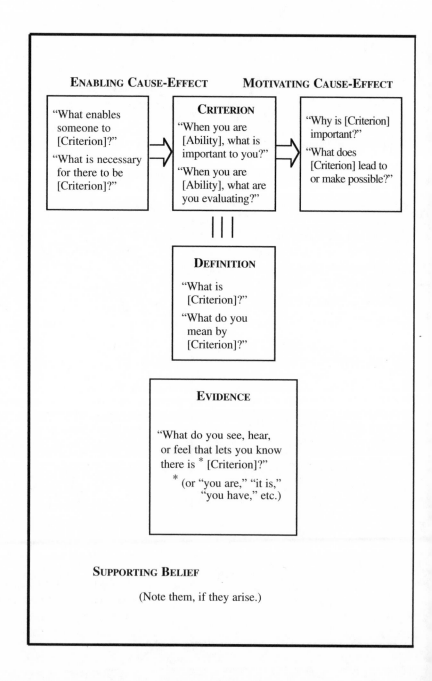

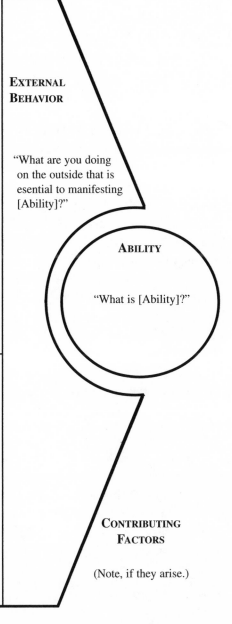

PRIMARY STRATEGY

"What are you usually doing - on the 'inside' and on the 'outside' - to [Ability]?"

"How do you normally go about [Ability]?"

SECONDARY STRATEGIES

"What do you do when that is not working well enough?"

"What do you do when that is not working at all?"

"What do you do when it cannot work?"

EXTERNAL BEHAVIOR

"What are you doing on the outside that is esential to manifesting [Ability]?"

ABILITY

"What is [Ability]?"

SUSTAINING EMOTION

"What is the background feeling that keeps you engaged in [Ability]?"

"When you are [Ability], what emotion is always operating in the background of your experience to help *keep* you [Ability]?"

SIGNAL EMOTIONS

(Note them as they arise.)

CONTRIBUTING FACTORS

(Note, if they arise.)

APPENDIX IV

LENNY: MAINTAINING A DIET TO CONTROL TYPE II DIABETES

We offer Lenny's model as an additional—and quite different—example of how the Experiential Array can be used to capture the essential patterns of experience that give rise to a particular Ability.

After not feeling well for months, Lenny found himself waking up in a hospital emergency room. He had collapsed while taking a walk. When the nurse heard that he had lost weight and had been craving water and sugar, she decided to check his blood glucose. "Now a normal reading for a fasting non-diabetic individual is somewhere between 70 and 120," Lenny explained. "And I was 533. The nurse says, 'You're diabetic. You're having a sugar crisis right now.' So they send me upstairs and start pumping me full of insulin, which changed my entire universe about fifteen minutes after the first injection."

Diagnosed as a Type II diabetic, Lenny was quickly educated about testing his blood and taking medication, a regimen he would have to follow the rest of his life. He did not like the idea of taking medication. When he later heard about a diet that had allowed other diabetics to keep their blood sugar stable, he decided to try it.[1] It worked. That was six years ago and Lenny has been maintaining his blood glucose levels since then through this diet. Impressed by his ability to stick to a demanding diet regimen for so many years, we decided to model him. You can find the Experiential Array that came out of that modeling is on pages 198 and 199.

Criterion

"Working" is not a surprising Criterion, and is probably similar to the Criteria that many people hold when trying to stick to a diet. What is tremendously significant about Lenny's particular form of the Criterion, however, is that it is expressed as "work*ing*," and not "works" or "worked."

---

[1] The diet Lenny follows was created by Dr. Barry Sears, and is described in detail in a number of publications, including Sears and Lawren's, *The Zone: A Dietary Road Map,* Harper Collins, 1995.

Lenny's "working" presupposes an ongoing evaluation; there is no end point to reach which, once attained, means he is done.

This contrasts with people who evaluate whether or not their diet "works" or has "worked." These Criteria place these people in a very different subjective situation from that of Lenny. When (for whatever reason) they hit a snag in their dieting, their evaluation is likely to be that the diet "*doesn't* work" or "*hasn't* worked." In both cases, the subjective experience is that there is something wrong with the diet (or "me"), and that *something has ended.* (Step into the situation of being on a diet while holding either one of those Criteria and notice out how it affects your feelings, thoughts, and choices.) Obviously, neither of these other orientations are supportive of continuing to follow a diet.

The structure of experience presupposed by "working," however, orients us in a fundamentally different way. When Lenny hits a snag there is no sense that the diet cannot work, just that it is not working *currently*. Also, there is less a sense that something is done, finished, or proven; instead there is more the sense of the need for adjustment. Both of these orientations strongly support an endless and ongoing effort, which is just what Lenny needs to maintain his diet regimen.

Definition

Lenny's Definition—"My blood is regulated and consistent"—is very much in line with what is suggested by the Criterion; the Definition describes something that is ongoing, rather than an event or end point. Again, that matters. Suppose instead that the experience you are evaluating as "working" has the quality of an event or end point, such as "My blood numbers are perfect," "My blood is controlled," or "I'm free of any symptoms." These experiences are much more likely to generate negative evaluations. The normal ebbs and flows of life, behavior, the weather, and blood chemistry ensure that your blood numbers will fluctuate. Each of these fluctuations and off moments would be seen as instances of the diet not working. And after enough instances of "it's not working," it becomes tempting to abandon the effort. (Actually, it is our experience that such Definitions are not likely to be labeled "working," but would carry a Criterial label that is more congruent with the subjective qualities of the Definition: for instance, the diet "works," I'm "healthy," or it's a "success.") The dynamic is the same as that of someone on a weight-loss diet who is evaluating whether or not he is "slim." The answer is *No* until he is slim. If it will take a year to get there, that is a

Lenny's Array

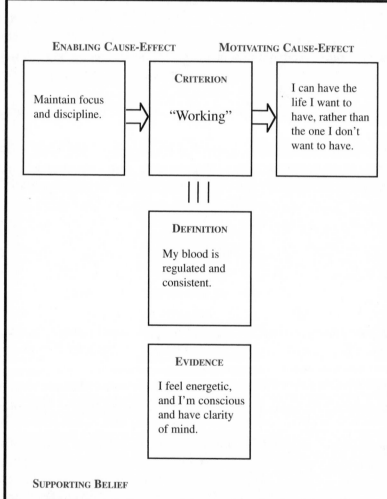

ENABLING CAUSE-EFFECT   **MOTIVATING CAUSE-EFFECT**

Maintain focus and discipline.

CRITERION

"Working"

I can have the life I want to have, rather than the one I don't want to have.

DEFINITION

My blood is regulated and consistent.

EVIDENCE

I feel energetic, and I'm conscious and have clarity of mind.

SUPPORTING BELIEF

"Insulin is really the enemy. It is more damaging than it is good, in excess amounts."

"I am a diabetic and I'm a diabetic for the rest of my life."

"The [dieting] system only exists because I remember that it does, and that I pay attention to it."

"Now I don't have anyone to rely on except myself."

PRIMARY STRATEGY

Follow the Zone Diet.

EXTERNAL BEHAVIOR

SECONDARY STRATEGIES

1. Remember being back in the hospital and just before, and feel mild panic.
2. Go into the negative future.
3. Go into the positive future and remember that: "If I'm going to get there, I need to follow the diet," and "I am one or two meals/steps away from getting back on track."
4. Feel stronger, back in control.
5. Go back to the beginning of the diet and follow it strictly until I'm back on track.

Talk about it a lot with other people.

ABILITY

Maintaining a Diet to Control Type II Diabetes

SUSTAINING EMOTION

Powerful / Strong

SIGNAL EMOTIONS

Mild Panic

CONTRIBUTING FACTORS

Understand the mechanics of food and of the body.

Celebrate the fact that I'm a Type II diabetic by taking a diet vacation for a day.

year's worth of *No*. That is a lot for anyone to endure, and can quickly become dispiriting.

The experience on which Lenny focuses his attention ("my blood is regulated and consistent"), however, suggests he is *monitoring and adjusting a range* within which he wants to keep his blood sugar. Even with the vagaries of life and blood chemistry, this means that most of the time his Criterion will be satisfied. Lenny's particular Definition of "working" gives him a lot of ongoing *Yes*es, and this naturally reinforces his efforts and supports his maintaining his diet.

Evidence

Lenny's Evidence—"I feel energetic, and I'm conscious and have clarity of mind"—puts his attention on his ongoing, internal experience, making him much more able to notice and respond to ongoing shifts in his blood sugar than someone whose evidence is the blood glucose number read-outs from sticking his finger periodically for blood tests.

Also, because his Evidence is internally generated he is not dependent upon the often capricious responses of the external world. For example, if his Evidence was "People tell me I'm looking good," he would be at the mercy of the world for feedback about how his diet was working. People may not notice that he is looking good, or they may but not comment on it, or one person may say he looks good and a minute later someone else says he does not. Instead, Lenny has his own, internal compass to tell him whether or not he is heading in the right direction with his diet.

In addition, because his Evidence is about the *quality* of his internal experience, he gets relatively frequent feedback about changes in his state and, so, is frequently faced with the need to do something in response to it. This helps keep the importance of his diet *present and real* for him.

Enabling Cause-Effect

At first, Lenny's Enabling Cause-Effect seems obvious. We might be tempted to consider it trivial because everyone knows you have to follow a diet to get its benefits. But does everyone *believe* that? Remember, when we speak of "believing" here, we are talking about those equivalence and causal relationships that actually give rise to our experiences, and that drive our behaviors. These are the beliefs that are *real* or *true* for us. We can know that one has to follow a diet to gain its benefits without that cause-effect being real for us; it is simply information, and has no effect on our behavior.

For Lenny, the causal connection between "maintaining the focus and discipline" on the diet and it "working" is not merely an idea or an imposed rule; it is real and true for him. It is also clear that many people trying to maintain a diet regimen (or any regimen, for that matter) do not have this same Enabling Cause-Effect operating. The consequence of this is both subtle and significant. Without this cause-effect the cause (the "agency") will not be considered to be the *person,* but the *diet itself.* It is the *diet* that causes the blood sugar to stabilize (or weight to be lost, or increased muscle mass, or better energy). And so, when the person finds that he is not meeting his intended goal (satisfying his Criterion), it is easy and natural to search for another diet, one that "works." For Lenny, however, discovering that his diet is not "working" means that *he* has not been adequately maintaining focus and discipline, and that *he* must resume them in order to get it working again. If all that sounds like a lot of effort, well, it is. To know what keeps Lenny—or anyone—pursuing his Criterion, we turn to the Motivating Cause-Effect.

Motivating Cause-Effect

In most present moments, Lenny is probably just fine. He feels energetic, conscious and clear; he feels good. It is also in the present that a pint of ice cream looks good. For most of us, feeling okay in the present *and* wanting the ice cream can lead to thoughts such as, "I'm feeling good, so maybe I don't need to be so careful today. And so what if I eat this ice cream now? It's just this once; no big deal. And I deserve a little pleasure." As long as the significance of eating the ice cream is evaluated in the time frame of the *present,* it is probably going to get eaten.

But of course it is through the choices in the present that we are creating the future. Lenny's Motivating Cause-Effect makes a direct connection between the choices he makes in the present regarding "maintaining the focus and discipline," the need to keep his diet "working," and his *future.* We all know that following the diet will be good for us, exercising will be good for us, smoking will be bad for us, and so on. But Lenny *believes* this; the experience of the causal connection between the working of his diet and his future is real to him. Because of that, when he considers straying from the diet (either because it is a burden in the moment, or because that moment is offering something very tempting), the connection between the present and the future *helps take him out of the present.* The choices of the present are extremely compelling. By adding a real sense of the future, the present compulsion is blunted and Lenny can choose based on a perspective that is driven by the needs of the future, rather than the desires of the present.

Furthermore, Lenny's Motivating Cause-Effect includes *both* the future he wants and the future he wants to avoid. This creates the subjective experience of moving toward the future he wants when his diet is working, and moving toward the future he does *not* want when his diet is *not* working. As we know from our own experience, avoiding unpleasantness is very motivating. For most of us, avoiding an unpleasant future is more immediately compelling than it is to move toward a pleasant future.

But then why have both? Why not simply have a cause-effect between the diet working and avoiding the unpleasant future? The reason is that continually having to avoid future unpleasantness can *itself* become oppressively unpleasant. This is what Lenny would be facing many times each day if he represented only the future he wants to avoid. If you try this out in your own experience you will probably find that you quickly get to the point of wanting to avoid (deny) the whole question of what you ought to be doing in the present—"To hell with the whole thing"—and giving up on the diet. Having a future to avoid is very motivating, but having *only* a future to avoid can become *de*motivating. By holding a cause-effect relationship between his diet working and both possible futures, Lenny has the impetus both of avoiding the unwanted future and of moving in the direction of the wanted future.

Supporting Beliefs

Lenny's Supporting Beliefs include:

"Insulin is really the enemy. It is more damaging than it is good, in excess amounts."

"I am a diabetic and I'm a diabetic for the rest of my life."

"The [dieting] system only exists because I remember that it does, and that I pay attention to it."

"Now I don't have anyone to rely on except myself."

For Lenny, these Supporting Beliefs are not bells and whistles that have been tacked onto his ability to maintain a diet. They are integral to the system dynamics. You can operate out of the essential equivalences and cause-effects in Lenny's Belief Template without believing that "insulin is the enemy," or that "I'm a diabetic for life." But the usefulness of any of these Supporting Beliefs becomes immediately evident when you hold them as you step into the context of being a diabetic who is wanting to stick to a diet.

Primary Strategy

Lenny's Primary Strategy is, of course, to follow the guidelines and steps laid out for him by the Zone diet. (In this case, since a description of the dieting strategy already exists in books, we did not feel it necessary to reproduce it in the Array.)

No matter why you are dieting, there is some dieting protocol that you need to follow if you want to have the effects of the diet. Most people are perfectly capable of following a diet...*in the beginning.* It often becomes difficult to stick to the diet as the days turn into weeks and the weeks into months. The heady and self-reinforcing successes of the initial days are often followed by missteps, feelings of deprivation, and frustrations that lead to such thoughts as, "I can't do this," "the diet isn't working," "it doesn't really matter if I don't follow it this once," "I can get serious about this next week," and so on. Regardless of the rationalization, the result is the same: the diet is dropped.

Successfully maintaining a diet regimen requires some way of effectively responding to these pitfalls. We want robust models, of course, models that withstand the often uncooperative vagaries of the real world. Much of this resiliency is the result of having effective Secondary Strategies, and this is where the particular genius of Lenny's Strategy is to be found.

Secondary Strategies

Like everyone else, there are times when Lenny either makes mistakes in following his diet, or rationalizes making choices that violate his diet. When he does, he will notice that he is feeling less energetic, conscious and clear (Evidence). Instead of responding to this (as so many of us do) by tumbling into a deep well of "It's no good" and "It's no use," Lenny responds with a Secondary Strategy that brings him right back into following his diet.

There are many brilliant aspects to his Secondary Strategy, but to talk about them it is helpful to first look at what is often going on when someone needs to follow a regimen (diet, exercise, quitting smoking, etc.), but it isn't going well.

Human beings generally try to avoid what is unpleasant. We go away from what is painful. The decision to embark on a diet (or exercise or health program) is very likely to be triggered by something that has become really unpleasant, something that you feel cannot be ignored and allowed to continue. So you start the diet. Then you are offered cheesecake, which you love and have not had in weeks, and you feel deprived; or you happen to be feeling unhappy and know that ice cream would be comforting; or you have gone two weeks without losing any weight and feel frustrated. Now your present experience is *again* unpleasant—"deprived," "unhappy," "frustrated"—and, naturally, you want to go away from *that*. Eating the cheesecake—dumping the diet—is a way of getting away from those *present* unpleasant feelings.

Lenny does something different, of course. By beginning with a recollection of the period of feeling physically terrible and ending up in the hospital, he brings into his experiential present the reality of what happens when he does not control his blood sugar. This is very different from what many people do who give up on a regimen. Like Lenny, they have had bad experiences (wheezing on a hike, having to buy larger clothes, fits of coughing), but unlike Lenny, these experiences are either not accessed, or are remembered only as information, as something that happened in the past. Lenny remembers *being in* the hospital, he is *there* again.

Many people who are trying to follow a regimen know what the future has in store for them if they do not stick with it: unable to get around, heart disease, lung cancer, etc. But again, that future is just information. It isn't real. By recapturing into his present experience the very real pain of the past (Step 1), Lenny gives himself the basis for a realistic—in fact, visceral—experience of what his future will be if he does not control his blood sugar (Step 2). These first two steps provide a real and compelling unpleasant (in fact, awful) future in response to the fact that his diet is *not* "Working." That future is something he really wants to avoid.

If all Lenny did was to scare himself with that awful future, it could quickly become something oppressive. Like everyone else, he would want to get away from that unpleasantness, and may well do so by dumping the diet. Instead, Lenny reminds himself of the future he *does* want (Step 3). This gives him something to go towards. This not only supports feelings such as hope, inspiration, and determination, but it also provides a direction for his efforts ("keeping to" the diet).

As we mentioned, generating the unpleasant future gives Lenny something to get away from. But there are a wide range of ways to get away: indulgent eating, going to sleep, giving up the diet, and so on. It is like wanting just to get out of town; no matter where else you go, at least you will be out of that town. But of course, you could wind up in another awful town. By recapturing the future he wants, Lenny is selecting the town he will go to. The unwanted future provides the impetus to move, the wanted future provides the worthwhile direction.

Even having the direction of that future may not be enough, however. It is still the future, something far from the present. Often people feel that they have gone so far off their diet that the future is suddenly as remote as it ever was, the task of getting there feels overwhelming, and they give up. Lenny, however, keeps his future within reach by reminding himself that, "I am one or two meals/steps away from getting back on track." This creates the subjective experience that what he needs to do in order to be back on his diet is *something relatively small and well within his grasp*.

He supports this renewed experience of the string of cause-effects that lead to his future by feeling stronger (Step 4), and then finally goes back to following his diet. But he does not return to where he *left off*. Obviously, he had been slipping in some way in following his diet regimen; otherwise things would still be "Working." So he returns to the focus and discipline of strictly following the diet (Step 5). This simultaneously reminds him of what he needs to do, and ensures that he gets back to feeling energetic, conscious and clear (satisfying his Criterion), which in turn reinforces the causal connections between these things, as well as providing him with a growing sense of control.

Lenny has no Secondary Strategies to deal with "Criterion not at all satisfied" or "Criterion cannot be satisfied." This makes sense. He cannot afford to be in those situations. To get to the point at which his diet is "not at all Working" or "cannot Work" is to be in a life-threatening situation (or at the very least, the situation of having to live on medications, which he really does not want to do.)

Sustaining Emotion

In "maintaining my diet to control my diabetes," Lenny's Sustaining Emotion is *powerful/strong*. Why is he using two words to identify what he is feeling? The infinite variety and shades of emotional experience will always outstrip language's ability to generate labels. It may be the case that the precise word an exemplar needs to describe a particular feeling simply does not exist, or is not known to him. When this happens, the quality of the exemplar's experience can usually be captured by combining two or more emotion labels. Lenny is feeling neither powerful nor strong, but some combination of the two emotions. They may seem very close. But if you compare them by taking on one then the other yourself, you will notice a subtle difference: *powerful* conveys a sense of being able to exert force or will, while *strong* conveys a sense of being able to withstand great forces:

Powerful: Like all diets, Lenny's diet is demanding. Many people soon feel inadequate to meet, or are overwhelmed by, these demands and give up ("I can't do it" "It's too hard"). As Lenny's beliefs make clear, the responsibility for the required effort is his. He must do the work, and it is not trivial work. The sense of being capable of making happen what he wants to happen that comes from feeling *powerful* helps sustain Lenny in doing what needs to be done to meet the demands of the diet.

Strong: Diets are, by definition, restrictive. They proscribe what you are used to eating and probably *want* to eat. Unlike *powerful*, which engenders a sense of being able to exert pressure, feeling *strong* conveys more of the sense of being able to withstand pressure. This quality of *strong* supports Lenny in holding constant to his diet in the face of daily temptations and entreaties from the world to stray from his commitment.

Diets are not only demanding, those demands are often *endless*. This is clearly the case with a diet to control diabetes, and may also be the case for people who are on diets to control other health concerns, such as blood pressure, cholesterol and weight. Lenny cannot lift the stone once, then dust off his hands and walk away. He must lift it again and again, perhaps for the rest of his life. He must endure. Here again feeling strong sustains him by conveying a sense of power that lasts, that goes through time.

As a Sustaining Emotion, then, feeling *powerful/strong* helps Lenny to feel capable of exerting his will (so he can do what needs to be done), to withstand forces exerted upon him (so he can avoid temptations to stray), and to endure (so he can continue doing what needs to be done and avoiding temptations).

External Behavior

We found one External Behavior that emerged as both significant and not necessarily an automatic consequence of taking on the internal structures of Lenny's experience: "I talk about it [dieting to control diabetes] a lot with other people." When you try on this behavior, you immediately discover its effect on, and importance to, the ability to maintain the diet. To begin with, talking a lot with other people about dieting to control his diabetes reinforces why he is doing it, strengthening the cause-effects and keeping in his awareness the causal connections between his present choices and his future. In addition, people very often praise him for what he is doing, and are obviously impressed and interested. This validates what he is doing and his efforts, as well as creating a community of support (which includes the social pressure of their expectation that he maintain his diet). And finally, each time he talks about what he is doing and why, it creates a re-commitment—a personal reaffirmation—to the difficult path he is on.

Contributing Factors

For Lenny, being able to "understand the mechanics of food and of the body" makes it much easier to understand how what he is doing with his diet relates to what is actually happening in his body. Because of his knowledge of the physiology at work, Lenny is not blindly following the dictates of a diet. Instead, those dictates *make sense to him.* Rules without reason are easily broken or discarded altogether. Rules that are not understood in terms of their cause-effects are more easily ignored because the consequences are neither obvious nor do they seem inevitable to the person. Because of his knowledge, however, the dietetic rules Lenny must follow have reasons that he understands; to ignore them becomes choosing to ignore what he knows to be *true,* and to invite the predictably grave consequences.

In addition, says Lenny, "[Understanding the mechanics of food and the body] allows me to be generative about how I pick foods." His knowledge frees him to go to restaurants or to the homes of friends for a meal because he can figure out from what is available how to eat in a way that is consistent with his diet.

A second Contributing Factor for Lenny is that once in awhile "I celebrate the fact that I'm a Type II diabetic by taking a diet vacation for a day." Although this may at first seem counter intuitive, Lenny's "diet vacation" contributes to his ability to stay on his diet in several ways:

* It provides periodic relief from the constant burden of watching what he eats.

* The effect of going off his diet (having his sense of "energy," "consciousness" and "clarity of mind" impaired) renews the reality of

the cause-effect between his eating and his health. (If one has been eating properly and, so, feeling fine, the reason why you are bothering to eat properly can fade; after all, you are feeling fine!)

* Taking a day off from the diet and then resuming it reinforces the essential notion that, "I am one or two meals/steps away from getting back on track." (Undoubtedly, putting himself "back on track" serves to enhance his feelings of being "powerful/strong," as well.)

* It is a "celebration" in that things could have been worse; had he been a Type I diabetic (or perhaps had some other illness), he would not have been able to even contemplate having such choices. As it is, he has room for error and some freedom to choose, and this *is* cause for celebration.

Despite these effects, isn't it dangerous to fall off the diet wagon, to invite the very slippage that so many people typically fight and succumb to when following diets? Perhaps, *if the person is not operating out of Lenny's structure of experience.* Remember that it is not just anyone taking this diet vacation; it is Lenny, with his beliefs, strategies and emotions. For example, even though he is taking the day off from his diet, it is still *real* for him that, "My diet needs to work if I am going to have the future I want and avoid the one I *don't* want." Someone else who does not have this cause-effect (for whom it is just words, and not subjectively real) may not have Lenny's experiential resources to resume the diet. For this person, taking the day off becomes something very different, something that is less of a vacation and more of an escape.

Bibliography

Ashby, W. Ross (1956) *An Introduction to Cybernetics*. London: Chapman & Hall Ltd.

Anderson, Walter Truett (1990) *Reality Isn't What It Used To Be*. San Francisco: Harper & Row.

Bandler, Richard and John Grinder (1975) *The Structure of Magic, Volume 1*. Palo Alto, CA: Science and Behavior Books, Inc.

Bandler, Richard and John Grinder (1975) *Patterns of the Hypnotic Techniques of Milton H. Erickson, M.D., Vol. 1*. Cupertino, CA: Meta Publications.

Bateson, Gregory (1966) Slippery theories. International Journal of Psychiatry. 2/4 pp.415-417.

Bateson, Gregory (1979) *Mind and Nature: A Necessary Unity*. New York: Bantam Books.

Bateson, Gregory (1972) *Steps to an Ecology of Mind*. New York: Ballantine Books.

Bateson, Gregory (1991) *A Sacred Unity: Further Steps to an Ecology of Mind*. New York: Harper Collins.

Bateson, Gregory and Mary Catherine Bateson (1987) *Angels Fear: Towards an Epistemology of the Sacred*. New York: Macmillan Publishing Company.

Bohm, David (1985) *Unfolding Meaning*. London: Ark Paperbacks.

Bohm, David (1989) Meaning and information. *The Search for Meaning: The New Spirit in Science and Philosophy*. Paavo Pylkkänen (ed.). Northamptonshire: Crucible.

Bohm, David (1994) *Thought as a System*. London: Routledge.

Bohm, David (1996) *On Dialogue*. London: Routledge.

Cameron-Bandler, Leslie, David Gordon and Michael Lebeau (1985) *Know How*. San Rafael, CA: FuturePace, Inc.

Cameron-Bandler, Leslie and Michael Lebeau (1986) *The Emotional Hostage*. San Rafael, CA: FuturePace, Inc.

Cameron-Bandler, Leslie, Michael Lebeau and David Gordon (1985) *The Emprint Method*. San Rafael, CA: FuturePace, Inc.

Clavell, James (1981) *The Children's Story*. New York: Dell Publishing.

Coulson, Seana (2000) *Semantic Leaps: Frame Shifting and Conceptual Blending in Meaning Construction.* New York and Cambridge: Cambridge University Press.

Csikszentmihalyi, Mihaly (1990) *Flow: the Psychology of Optimal Experience.* New York: Harper & Row.

Damasio, Antonio (1999) *The Feeling of What Happens: Body and Emotion in the Making of Consciousness.* New York: Harcourt Brace & Company.

Darwin, Charles (1872) *The Expression of the Emotions in Man and Animals.* Chicago: University of Chicago Press (1965).

Dawes, Graham (1997) "The Significance of Neuro-Linguistic Programming in the Therapy of Anxiety Disorders". Clinical Management of Anxiety. Johan A. den Boer (ed.). New York: Marcel Dekker Inc.

Dawes, Graham (1999) "Faster Than a Speeding Bullet: The Quick Change Speed Trials". Anchor Point. Vol. 13, No. 2.

Dawes, Graham and John Killman (2000) "The Excellent Auditor". Qualityworld. Institute of Quality Assurance. Vol. 26, Issue 3.

Depraz, Natalie, Francisco Varela, and Pierre Vermersch (eds.) (2003) *On Becoming Aware: A Pragmatics of Experiencing.* Amsterdam/Philadelphia: John Benjamins Publisahing Company.

Diamond, Jared (1984) "Race Without Color". Discover Magazine. pp.82-89.

Dilts, Robert, John Grinder, Richard Bandler, Leslie Cameron Bandler and Judith DeLozier (1980) *Neuro-Linguistic Programming: Volume 1.* Cupertino, CA: Meta Publications.

Edelman, Gerald (1992) *Bright Air, Brilliant Fire.* New York: BasicBooks.

Edwards, Betty (1999) *The New Drawing on the Right Side of the Brain.* New York: Jeremy P. Tarcher/Putnam.

Elbow, Peter (1986) *Embracing Contraries.* New York: Oxford University Press.

Fauconnier, Gilles (1994/1985) *Mental Spaces: Aspects of Meaning Construction in Natural Language.* Second edition. Cambridge: Cambridge University Press.

Fauconnier, Gilles and Mark Turner (2002) *The Way We Think: Conceptual Blending and the Mind's Hidden Complexity.* Basic Books, New York.

Festinger, Leon, Henry W. Riecken, and Stanley Schachter (1956) *When Prophecy Fails.* Minneapolis: University of Minnesota Press.

Feyerabend Paul (1978) *Against Method.* London: Verso.

Foerster, Heinz von (1979) Cybernetics of cybernetics, *Communication and Control in Society.* Klaus Krippendorff (ed.). New York: Gordon and Breach.

Foerster, Heinz von (1991) Through the eyes of the other. *Research and*

Reflexivity. Frederick Steier (ed.). London: Sage Publications.

Frankl, Victor (1984) *Man's Search for Meaning.* New York: Washington Square Press.

Gordon, David (1990) "Reference Experiences: Guardians of Coherence and Instigators of Change". *Brief Therapy: Myths, Methods, and Metaphors.* Zeig and Gilligan (eds.) New York: Brunner/Mazel.

Gordon, David (1988) "The Role of Language in Therapy". *Developing Ericksonian Therapy.* Zeig and Lankton (eds.). New York: Brunner/Mazel.

Gordon, David (1985) "The Role of Presuppositions in Ericksonian Psychotherapy". *Ericksonian Psychotherapy, Volume I: Structures.* Zeig (ed.). New York: Brunner/Mazel.

Gordon, David and Maribeth Meyers-Anderson (1981) *Phoenix: Therapeutic Patterns of Milton H. Erickson.* Cupertino, CA: Meta Publications.

Gould, Stephen Jay (1996) *Full House: The Spread of Excellence from Plato to Darwin.* New York: Three Rivers Press.

Grandin, Temple (1996) *Thinking in Pictures.* New York: Vintage Books.

Haley, Jay (1973) *Uncommon Therapy: The Psychiatric Techniques of Milton H. Erickson, M.D.* New York: W.W. Norton & Company.

Hall, Edward T. (1959) *The Silent Language.* New York: Doubleday & Company.

Hall, Edward T. (1966) *The Hidden Dimension.* Garden City, NY: Anchor Books.

Hall, Edward T. (1976) *Beyond Culture.* Garden City, NY: Anchor Press/Doubleday.

Hall, Edward T. (1983) *The Dance of Life.* Garden City, NY: Anchor Press/Doubleday.

Jaynes, Julian (1976) *The Origin of Consciousness in the Breakdown of the Bicameral Mind.* Boston: Houghton Mifflin Company.

Johnson, Mark (1987) *The Body in the Mind: The Bodily Basis of Meaning, Imagination, and Reason.* Chicago: University of Chicago Press.

Keeney, Bradford P. (1983) *Aesthetics of Change.* New York: The Guilford Press.

Koornhof, Piet (2001) "The Makings of Genius". The Strad. Vol. 112, No. 1338.

Korzybski, Alfred (1958) *Science and Sanity.* Lakeville, Connecticut: The International Non-Aristotelian Library Publishing Company.

Korzybski, Alfred (1951) "The Role of Language in the Perceptual Processes". *Perception: An Approach to Personality.* Robert R. Blake and Glenn V. Ramsey (eds.). New York: The Ronald Press Company.

Kuhn, Thomas S. (1970) *The Structure of Scientific Revolutions.* Chicago: University of Chicago Press.

Lakoff, George (1987) *Women, Fire, and Dangerous Things: What Categories*

Reveal About the Mind. Chicago: University of Chicago Press.

Lakoff, George (1988) *Cognitive Semantics. Meaning and Mental Representations.* Umberto Eco, Marco Santambrogio and Patrizia Violi (eds.). Bloomington: Indiana University Press.

Lakoff, George and Mark Johnson (1980) *Metaphors We Live By.* Chicago: The University of Chicago Press.

Lakoff, George and Mark Johnson (1999) *Philosophy in the Flesh: The Embodied Mind and Its Challenge to Western Thought.* New York: Basic Books.

Lakoff, George and Mark Turner (1989) *More Than Cool Reason: A Field Guide to Poetic Metaphor.* Chicago: University of Chicago Press.

LeDoux, Joseph (1998) *The Emotional Brain.* London: Weidenfeld & Nicolson.

MacDonald, Celia and Steve Nuttall (2000) "Team Magic: An Exploration of Competencies and Abilities in Team Working". The National Training Organization for Oil and Gas Extraction. Internal report.

Maruyama, Magorah (1968) The second cybernetics: Deviation-amplifying mutual causal processes. *Modern Systems Research for the Behavioral Scientist.* W. Buckley (ed.). Chicago: Aldine.

Maturana, Humberto (1987) Everything is said by an observer. *Gaia: A Way of Knowing.* William Irwin Thompson (ed.). Great Barrington, MA: Lindisfarne Press.

Maturana, Humberto (1988) Reality: The search for objectivity or the quest for a compelling argument. The Irish Journal of Psychology. 9/1 pp.25-82.

Maturana, Humberto and Francisco Varela (1987) *The Tree of Knowledge.* Boston: New Science Library.

McCloud, Scott (1993) *Understanding Comics: The Invisible Art.* New York: Harper Perennial.

Miller, George A., Eugene Galanter, and Karl H. Pribram (1960) *Plans and the Structure of Behavior.* New York: Holt, Rinehart and Winston, Inc.

O'Hanlon, Bill and James Wilk (1987) *Shifting Contexts: The Generation of Effective Psychotherapy.* New York: The Guilford Press.

Ornstein, Robert and David Sobel (1987) *The Healing Brain.* New York: Simon & Schuster Inc.

Pearce, W. Barnett (1989) *Communication and the Human Condition.* Carbondale: Southern Illinois University Press.

Pearce, W. Barnett and Vernon E. Cronen (1980) *Communication, Action, and Meaning: The Creation of Social Realities.* New York: Praeger.

Penfield, Wilder and Phanor Perot (1963) "The Brain's Record of Auditory and Visual Experience". Brain. vol. 86, part 4.

Pert, Candace B. (1997) *Molecules of Emotion.* New York: Touchstone.

Petitmengin-Peugeot, Claire (1999) "The Intuitive Experience". *The View from Within: First-Person Approaches to the Study of Consciousness.* Francisco Varela and Jonathan Shear (eds.). Thorverton, UK: Imprint Academic.

Pylkkänen, Paavo (ed.) (1989) *The Search for Meaning: the New Spirit in Science and Philosophy.* Northamptonshire: Crucible.

Rheingold, Howard (1988) *They Have a Word For It : A Lighthearted Lexicon of Untranslatable Words & Phrases.* Los Angeles: Jeremy P. Tarcher, Inc.

Rose, Steven (1973) *The Conscious Brain.* New York: Alfred A. Knopf.

Sachs, Oliver (1995) *An Anthropologist on Mars.* New York: Alfred A. Knopf.

Thompson, William Irwin (1989) *Imaginary Landscapes: Making Worlds of Myth and Science.* New York: St. Martin's Press.

Turner, Mark (2001) *Cognitive Dimensions of Social Science: The Way We Think About Politics, Economics, Law, and Society.* Oxford University Press, New York.

Turner, Mark (1996) *The Literary Mind: The Origins of Thought and Language.* Oxford University Press, New York and Oxford.

Vaihinger, H. (1924) *The Philosophy of "As If".* London: Routledge, Kegan and Paul, Ltd.

Varela, Francisco J. (1987) Laying down a path in walking. *Gaia: A Way of Knowledge.* William Erwin Thompson (ed.). Great Barrington, MA: Lindisfarne Press.

Varela, Francisco J. (1992) The reenchantment of the concrete. *Zone 6: Incorporations.* Jonathan Crary and Sanford Kwinter (eds.). New York: Zone.

Varela, Francisco, Evan Thompson, and Eleanor Rosch (1997) *The Embodied Mind.* Cambridge, MA: The MIT Press.

Watzlawick, Paul (1984) *The Invented Reality.* New York: W.W. Norton.

Watzlawick, Paul, John Weakland, and Richard Fisch (1974) *Change: Principles of Problem Formation and Problem Resolution.* New York: W.W. Norton & Company.

Whorf, Benjamin Lee. (1964) *Language, Thought, and Reality.* Boston: The MIT Press.

Zeig, Jeffrey K. (1980) *A Teaching Seminar with Milton H. Erickson.* New York: Brunner/Mazel.